ANCHOR OF RESOLVE

A History of U.S. Naval Forces
Central Command/Fifth Fleet

Robert J. Schneller Jr.

NAVAL HISTORICAL CENTER
DEPARTMENT OF THE NAVY
WASHINGTON 2007

"Without a decisive naval force we can do nothing definitive, and with it, everything honorable and glorious."

—GEORGE WASHINGTON
TO MARQUIS DE LAFAYETTE,
15 NOVEMBER 1781.

CONTENTS

AREA OF
RESPONSIBILITY

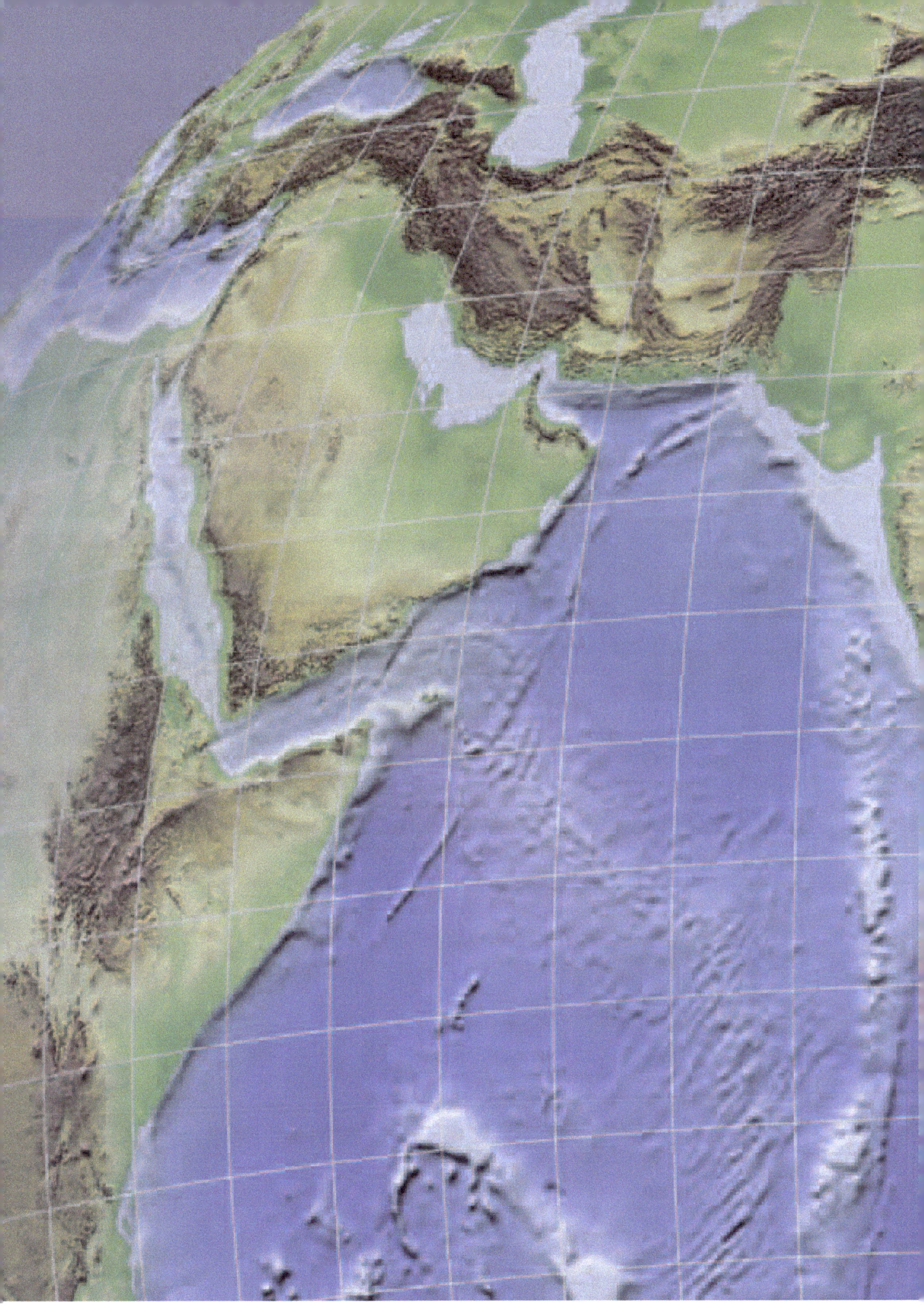

Lieutenant Commander Robert Lacy signals the launch of an F/A-18C Hornet for a mission in support of Operation Iraqi Freedom, 4 September 2004.

FOREWORD

The Naval Historical Center completed this illustrated history of U.S. Naval Forces Central Command/Fifth Fleet to accompany the exhibit it installed in the headquarters building on board Naval Support Activity Bahrain. In keeping with the Center's mission of supporting the operating forces, the purpose of this book is to inform visitors to the headquarters and American Sailors serving in the Middle East about the Navy's presence in Arabian waters and the variety of missions the Navy has conducted there, in peace and in war.

From the presidency of George Washington through the beginning of the Cold War, Americans have forged and maintained ties with the peoples of the Middle East. These bonds strengthened in 1949 with the establishment of the Middle East Force and a permanent U.S. naval presence in the Arabian Gulf. They grew even stronger when America committed itself to the defense of its friends in the region, establishing Central Command and its naval component, Naval Forces Central Command, in 1983. The United States Navy remains an anchor of resolve in promoting peace, stability, and prosperity in the Central Command area of responsibility.

The author, Dr. Robert J. Schneller Jr., is well qualified to present this informative and well-illustrated history. He is co-author of a book on the Navy's role in Operations Desert Shield and Desert Storm, and since 9/11 has been researching and writing about the Navy's role in the Global War on Terrorism. As with each of our histories, the views expressed herein are those of the author alone and not those of U.S. Naval Forces Central Command/Fifth Fleet, the Department of the Navy, or any other U.S. government agency.

Rear Admiral P. E. Tobin, U.S. Navy (Ret.)
Director of Naval History

Crown Prince Saud bin Abdul Aziz presents a gift to Captain R. W. Ruble during the visit of Valley Forge *(CV 45) to the Arabian Gulf, March 1948. The ship was the first U.S. carrier to enter the gulf.*

The oiler USNS Supply *(T-AOE 6) conducts an underway replenishment in the Arabian Gulf with the cruiser* Vella Gulf *(CG 72), 30 June 2004. The carrier* George Washington *(CVN 73) steams in the background.*

Aramco's refinery at Ras Tanura, Saudi Arabia, December 1952. That year the refinery produced 170,000 barrels of petroleum per day.

CHRONOLOGY

1833, September 21	United States and Muscat sign treaty of amity and commerce.
1945, February 14	President Franklin D. Roosevelt and King Abdul Aziz Ibn Saud meet on board cruiser *Quincy*.
1949, August 16	Navy establishes Middle East Force.
1968, July 17	Baath party seizes power in Iraq in a coup.
1971, December 23	The U.S. Navy takes over part of the former British naval base at Juffair, naming the facility Administrative Support Unit Bahrain.
1979, July 16	Saddam Hussein becomes president of Iraq.
1979, November 4	Iranian fundamentalist revolutionaries seize the U.S. Embassy in Tehran and hold its staff hostage for 444 days.
1979, December 27	Soviet Union invades Afghanistan.
1980, January 23	President Carter enunciates doctrine that commits American military forces to the defense of the Arabian Gulf region.
1980, March 1	Department of Defense establishes the Rapid Deployment Joint Task Force.
1980, September 22	Iraq invades Iran, launching an eight-year war.
1983, January 1	Department of Defense establishes U.S. Central Command (CENTCOM) and its naval component, U.S. Naval Forces Central Command (NAVCENT).
1987, March 7	U.S. government authorizes Kuwaiti tankers to sail under U.S. registry, and Operation Earnest Will escort missions begin.
1987, May 17	Iraqi Miraqe jet fires two Exocet missiles at the frigate *Stark*, nearly sinking the ship.
1987, July 1	Department of Defense establishes U.S. Transportation Command.
1987, August 21	Department of Defense establishes Joint Task Force Middle East.
1988, April 14	Frigate *Samuel B. Roberts* hits an Iranian mine in the Arabian Gulf.
1988, April 18	Navy launches Operation Praying Mantis and destroys half of Iran's operational navy.
1990, August 2	Iraq invades Kuwait.
1990, August 6	United States launches Operation Desert Shield.
1991, January 5	Following a coup in Somalia, NAVCENT forces conduct Operation Eastern Exit, evacuating 281 people from the U.S. Embassy in the capital, Mogadishu.
1991, January 17	Coalition forces launch Operation Desert Storm air and naval campaigns.
1991, February 24	Coalition forces launch Desert Storm ground campaign to drive Iraqi forces from Kuwait.
1991, February 28	Coalition forces cease offensive operations against Iraqi forces.

1991, April 5	Coalition forces launch Operation Provide Comfort and establish a "no-fly" zone over northern Iraq.
1992, June 25	Administrative Support Unit Bahrain is renamed Administrative Support Unit Southwest Asia.
1992, August 26	The United States, Great Britain, and France establish a no-fly zone over southern Iraq and U.S. forces launch Operation Southern Watch the next day; the CENTCOM commander establishes Joint Task Force Southwest Asia to manage Operation Southern Watch and to plan for other contingencies.
1992, August 28	CENTCOM launches Operation Provide Relief to deliver humanitarian aid to Somalia.
1992, December 4	Department of Defense launches Operation Restore Hope to facilitate U.N. peacekeeping efforts in Somalia.
1993, January 13	U.S., British, and French aircraft attack Iraqi air defense system in southern no-fly zone in response to Iraqi attacks on aircraft engaged in Operation Southern Watch.
1993, January 17	U.S. surface ships launch Tomahawk missiles against the Zaafaraniyah factory complex near Baghdad in response to Iraqi attacks on coalition aircraft patrolling the northern no-fly zone.
1993, April 10	COMUSNAVCENT flagship *La Salle* departs area of responsibility and COMUSNAVCENT staff move ashore to quarters in Bahrain.
1993, June 26	U.S. surface ships launch Tomahawk missiles against an Iraqi intelligence headquarters in Baghdad in response to an Iraqi assassination attempt on former President George H.W. Bush.
1993, October 3	Task Force Ranger launches its seventh operation in Mogadishu against warlord Mohammed Farah Aideed, during which two U.S. helicopters are shot down and 18 American soldiers killed.
1994, March 25	U.S. forces complete withdrawal from Somalia.
1994, October 7	U.S. forces begin surging to CENTCOM area of responsibility in response to buildup of Iraqi forces on the border with Kuwait.
1995, March 3	U.S. forces complete Operation United Shield, covering the withdrawal of U.N. peacekeepers from Somalia.
1995, July 1	Navy stands up U.S. Fifth Fleet.
1995, November 13	Al-Qaeda-associated terrorist car bomb explodes in Riyadh outside the Office of Program Management of the American-trained Saudi Arabian National Guard, killing seven people.
1996, January 1	Department of Defense adds to the CENTCOM area of responsibility the entire Arabian Sea and a portion of the Indian Ocean.
1996, June 26	Al-Qaeda terrorists bomb the Khobar Towers housing complex in Dhahran, Saudi Arabia.

1996, September 4	In Operation Desert Strike, U.S. ships and aircraft launch cruise missiles against surface-to-air missile and command and control facilities in southern Iraq, in response to an Iraqi attacks on the Kurdish city of Irbil and coalition aircraft in the southern no-fly zone; the United States and the United Kingdom also expand the southern no-fly zone from the 32nd to the 33rd parallel and promise a disproportionate response if the Iraqis repair the damaged air defense sites.
1998, January 18	CENTCOM launches Operation Desert Thunder, a large-scale deployment of U.S. and coalition forces to pressure Iraq into compliance with U.N. weapons inspectors.
1998, August 7	Al-Qaeda terrorists detonate truck bombs nearly simultaneously outside the U.S. embassies in the East African capitals of Nairobi, Kenya, and Dar es Salaam, Tanzania, killing more than 200 people.
1998, August 20	U.S. ships launch Operation Infinite Response, a simultaneous cruise missile strike against the Zhawar Kili al-Badr terrorist facilities in Afghanistan, and the al-Shifa pharmaceutical plant in Sudan, thought to be producing a precursor for the deadly VX nerve gas for al-Qaeda, in retaliation for the 7 August embassy attacks.
1998, December 16	In response to Iraqi noncompliance with U.N. weapons inspectors, CENTCOM launches Operation Desert Fox, a four-day punitive air campaign against Iraqi installations thought to be associated with developing weapons of mass destruction, units providing security to such programs, and Iraq's national command and control and air defense networks.
1999, August 5	Administrative Support Unit Southwest Asia is redesignated Naval Support Activity Bahrain.
2000, October 12	Al-Qaeda suicide operatives detonate boat bomb alongside the U.S. destroyer *Cole* during a brief refueling stop in Aden, Yemen, killing 17 Sailors and wounding 40.
2001, September 11	Al-Qaeda suicide operatives crashed hijacked passenger airliners into the World Trade Center towers in New York City, the Pentagon in Washington, and a field near Shanksville, Pennsylvania, killing nearly 3,000 people.
2001, October 7	U.S. forces launch Operation Enduring Freedom to remove the Taliban regime and destroy al-Qaeda forces and infrastructure in Afghanistan.
2001, December 7	Kandahar, the last major Taliban stronghold in Afghanistan, surrendered to Northern Alliance forces under the command of future Afghan President Hamid Karzai.
2003, March 19	Coalition forces launch Operation Iraqi Freedom to remove the Saddam Hussein regime from Iraq.
2003, April 9	Organized Iraqi resistance in Baghdad collapses.
2003, May 1	President George W. Bush announces the end of major combat operations in Iraq; Secretary of Defense Donald Rumsfeld declares the end of major combat operations in Afghanistan.

Electrician's Mate 2nd Class Chris Grahm stands ready to embark on a mission to clear shipping lanes for humanitarian relief operations in the Arabian Gulf, 17 March 2003.

INTRODUCTION

AMERICA'S INTERESTS IN THE MIDDLE EAST, Southwest Asia, and eastern Africa date almost to the founding of the nation. Since World War II, the United States Navy has been the first line of defense for these interests. From the establishment of the Middle East Force in 1949 through the beginning of the twenty-first century, the U.S. Navy served as a force for stability and peace in the region. The Navy's presence helped prevent regional crises from escalating into wars, enforce international sanctions, and minimize damage done by regional conflicts to American and allied interests. When there has been no other alternative, the Navy has gone to war by sea, air, and land to defend these interests. The Navy's presence also resulted in peaceful operations such as humanitarian assistance, maritime rescue, and military exercises with regional allies.

Early in the twenty-first century, the U.S. Naval Forces Central Command/Fifth Fleet area of responsibility encompassed about 7.5 million square miles of the earth's surface, including the Arabian Gulf, North Arabian Sea, Gulf of Oman, Gulf of Aden, Red Sea, and parts of the Indian Ocean. This expanse comprised 27 countries and three critical chokepoints at the Strait of Hormuz, the Suez Canal, and the Bab al-Mandeb at the southern tip of Yemen.

The Navy owes its success in this region to the patriotism, professionalism, pride, hard work, and self-sacrifice of the officers and enlisted men and women assigned to U.S. Naval Forces Central Command/Fifth Fleet. This is their story.

The screw sloop Ticonderoga *at Venice, Italy, circa 1866–1869. When this ship passed through the Strait of Hormuz in 1879, it became the first American man-of-war to sail in the gulf.*

GROWING AMERICAN INTERESTS

AFTER THE UNITED STATES WON INDEPENDENCE in 1783, American merchants sought broader opportunities in every corner of the globe. Although Great Britain remained the predominant naval power in the Indian Ocean throughout the nineteenth century, enterprising Americans soon reached markets on the subcontinent of India, along the east coast of Africa, on the Arabian Peninsula, and in the Arabian Gulf. Because the fundamental mission of the United States Navy has always been to protect American interests around the world, U.S. warships followed the flag of merchant sailors who pursued dreams of riches in Asia. With Great Britain's Royal Navy and maritime law protecting free trade in the Indian Ocean, Arabian Sea, and Arabian Gulf, the Navy only occasionally showed the flag in those waters during the nineteenth century.

The first U.S. warship to enter the Indian Ocean was the frigate *Essex*, which twice rounded the Cape of Good Hope in 1800 to escort a convoy of merchant ships returning from the Dutch East Indies. The Navy conducted its first operation off the Arabian Peninsula in 1833, when the sloop-of-war *Peacock* and the schooner *Boxer* carried an American diplomatic mission to Oman, an important hub for Indian Ocean trade. The mission culminated in a treaty of amity and commerce with Sultan Saiyid Said of Muscat.

The steam sloop *Ticonderoga* became the first American warship to sail into the Arabian Gulf after transiting the Strait of Hormuz in December 1879. Her presence constituted a long-delayed response to an invitation from the Shah of Persia, with whom the United States had signed a trade treaty in 1856. Under Commodore Robert Wilson Shufeldt, who was en route to Asia on an ultimately successful mission to open Korea to American commerce, *Ticonderoga* stopped at Bushehr and Basra and steamed 70 miles up the Shatt-al-Arab. Shufeldt found that American commercial interests constituted two-thirds of Muscat's trade. He also discovered that Arabs, Turks, and Persians liked the idea of another power helping to ameliorate the effects of "aggressive" British policy in the gulf,

which Great Britain had developed in the context of its "great game" with Russia for imperial hegemony in the region to protect trade routes to India.

Western interest in the Middle East increased significantly during the twentieth century, when petroleum supplanted coal as the fuel of choice for industrial nations. In 1901, British financier William Knox D'Arcy gained an oil concession covering nearly all of Persia. The first major strike seven years later at Masjid-i-Suleiman in western Persia heralded the beginning of the oil age in the Arabian Gulf. The British government's interest in the region heightened on the eve of World War I, when Winston Churchill, then First Lord of the Admiralty, decided to base the country's "naval supremacy upon oil." Thereafter the Royal Navy began replacing coal-burning engines in its warships with more efficient and economical oil-burning engines. With no known oil reserves of its own, Britain's naval power came to rest on Middle East petroleum.

Although the United States produced most of the world's oil between the world wars, American companies invested in British petroleum concessions in Iran and Kuwait, took over the concession in Bahrain, and established an all-American concession in Saudi Arabia. Oil production in the region increased 900 percent between 1920 and 1939, as

Bahrain, Saudi Arabia, and Iraq joined Iran as major producers. In 1920 less than 5 percent of the world's oil was produced outside the United States; by 1939 the figure had climbed to 14 percent.

American strategic interest in the region rose considerably during World War II, as German forces sought to drive east from Libya through British-controlled Egypt and link up with Nazi tanks driving south from the Soviet Union through the oil-rich Caucasus. After Britain, Russia, and Iran signed a treaty in January 1942, Iran served as a major corridor through which the U.S. government shipped supplies to the Soviet Union under the Lend Lease program. Approximately 4,159,117 tons of aircraft, vehicles, guns, ammunition, food, and other supplies and equipment reached Russia through Iran, nearly 25 percent of the total cargo shipped to the Soviet Union from the Western Hemisphere during the war. British, Russian, and American troops occupied Iran for the duration, with the U.S. Army presence peaking at nearly 30,000 men. The United States provided Lend Lease support to Saudi Arabia as well.

Well number seven at Dammam, Saudi Arabia, spewing oil, 1938.

The war highlighted the latent strategic importance of Middle East petroleum. In 1943, geologists estimated that the proven and probable reserves in Bahrain, Kuwait, Qatar, Saudi Arabia, Iraq, and Iran numbered approximately 25 billion to 300 billion barrels of oil. For Saudi Arabia alone, estimates ranged from 5 billion to 100 billion barrels. One leading geologist predicted that "the center of gravity of world oil production" would soon shift from the Gulf of Mexico to the Arabian Gulf. Indeed, the postwar economies of the free world would come to depend on Middle Eastern oil.

On the way home from the February 1945 conference in Yalta, President Franklin D. Roosevelt entertained King Farouk of Egypt, Emperor Haile Selassie of Ethiopia, and King Abdul Aziz Ibn Saud of Saudi Arabia. The meetings took place on board the heavy cruiser *Quincy* (CA 71), anchored in Egypt's Great Bitter Lake on the Suez Canal.

The meeting with King Saud, as President Roosevelt later put it, "was perfectly amazing." The President had arranged for the destroyer *Murphy* (DD 603) to carry the King and his retinue from Jeddah, the port of the holy city of Mecca on the Red Sea, to the Great Bitter Lake. As the destroyer approached the cruiser, the sight of the royal entourage on the deck of *Murphy*, according to one observer, seemed like "a spectacle out of the past." Royal bodyguards armed with long rifles and unsheathed scimitars lined the forecastle, while the King sat in an ornate antique French chair atop a great pile of Oriental rugs on the forward gun deck. A tent for housing the King and his retinue of more than forty people stood on the bow as a flock of sheep for their food milled about on the stern.

The meeting began amicably. King Saud, who had received nine wounds in battle and walked with a noticeable limp, expressed interest in Roosevelt's wheelchair. In a personal gesture, Roosevelt gave the King one of his wheelchairs, as well as a state gift of a C-47 aircraft. Ibn Saud bestowed upon the President rich robes, perfumes, and a sword in a diamond-studded scabbard.

Tension grew, however, as the discussion turned toward the settlement of Jews in Palestine because the two leaders held opposite views on the issue. Sensing that Arabs and Jews were on a collision course, Roosevelt planned to reevaluate America's Palestine policy in search of a formula to prevent warfare, but didn't live long enough to do so. Nevertheless, the meeting demonstrated to King Saud that the United States might well play a more prominent role in the region. The meeting came to symbolize America's growing interest in the Middle East.

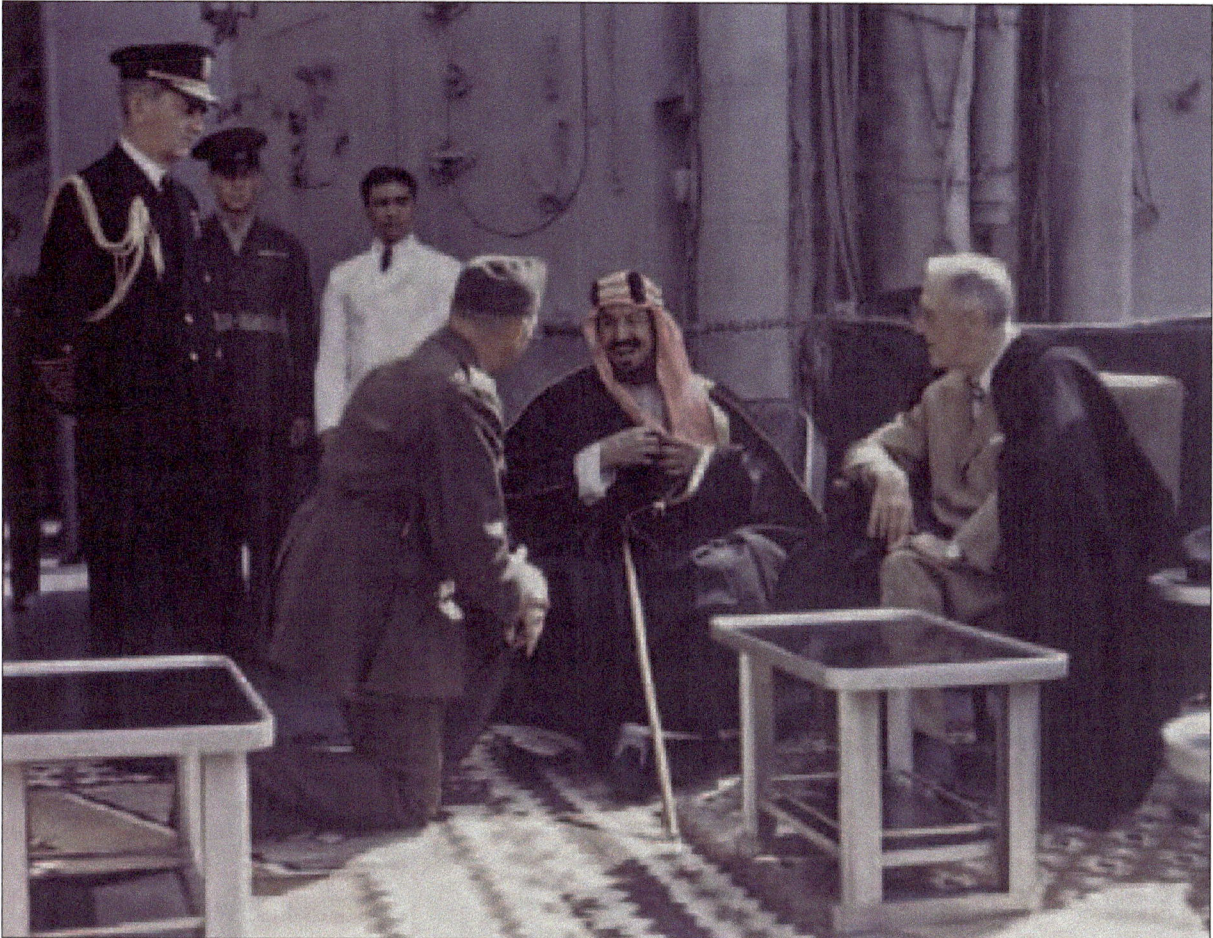

President Franklin D. Roosevelt and King Abdul Aziz Ibn Saud confer on board Quincy *(CA 71). Their meeting symbolized the growing importance of the region to America.*

The Cold War ushered in a new sense of urgency in Washington with regard to Middle East diplomacy. During World War II, the United States had been allied with Soviet dictator Joseph Stalin against a common enemy, Nazi Germany. By the spring of 1946, however, U.S. leaders had concluded that Stalin was bent on exporting Communist revolution worldwide and on advancing historical Russian interests along the Soviet Union's European and Asian periphery. Determined to counter these threats to world peace, U.S. leaders adopted a strategy of "containment." America and its allies would oppose the encroachment of the Soviet Union and its allies wherever it might occur.

The Cold War's first crisis emerged in the Middle East. Stalin not only refused to withdraw his troops from Iran within six months of the end of World War II as he had promised, but also set up the Communist Republic of Azerbaijan in northwest Iran. The United States and Britain pressured the Russians into pulling out of Iran by the end of May 1946, and the Soviet-sponsored Azeri regime soon collapsed.

The Iranian crisis marked a major departure in American foreign policy. President Harry S. Truman, who likened President Roosevelt's negotiations with the Soviets to appeasement, grew tired of "babying" the Russians and decided that it was time to "get tough." He convinced Congress that the United States should "support free peoples who are resisting subjugations by armed minorities or by outside pressure." Pundits dubbed this policy the Truman Doctrine.

The security of the Middle East would remain one of America's primary strategic interests throughout the Cold War and beyond. +++

ESTABLISHMENT OF THE MIDDLE EAST FORCE

WITH THE CREATION OF THE MIDDLE EAST FORCE (MEF) in 1949, the Navy assumed the role as the first line of defense for America's interests in the region. The founding of the Middle East Force also marked the transition of the Navy's presence in the Arabian Gulf from periodic to permanent.

In the years immediately following World War II, the Arabian Gulf became an area of vital concern to the Navy. American naval forces based in the Mediterranean and the Western Pacific after World War II burned fuel produced almost exclusively in the gulf region. As U.S. fleet oilers and chartered tankers began moving as many as 5 million barrels of petroleum products per month from the gulf to the Mediterranean and Pacific, the Navy perceived a need to establish facilities and a command and control structure to manage the traffic. Accordingly, on 20 January 1948 the Navy established Task Force (TF) 126 to control the dozens of ships plying gulf waters and operating out of Bahrain and Saudi Arabia. In subsequent months, this command evolved through several iterations and, on 16 August 1949, it was designated the Middle East Force. The Navy has maintained a continuous presence in the region ever since.

Under the command of a one-star admiral, the Middle East Force soon included a flagship, a pair of destroyers, aircraft, and support vessels. Between 1949 and 1965, duty as MEF flagship rotated among seaplane tenders *Duxbury Bay* (AVP 38), *Greenwich Bay* (AVP 41), and *Valcour* (AVP 55), each painted white to deflect the intense heat of the Arabian sun. In 1950, the U.S. Navy leased office space from the British naval base at Juffair, located five miles southeast of Manama, the capital of Bahrain. After the Navy reclassified *Valcour* as a miscellaneous

Middle East Force flagship Duxbury Bay *(AVP 38), mid-1960s.*

command flagship (AGF 1) and homeported her in Juffair in 1966, the ship served for six years as command post, living facility, and communications center for Commander Middle East Force and his staff of 15 officers. That same year MEF ships made 128 visits to 34 ports located in 12 countries and 6 protectorates or possessions, while the flag aircraft logged 77,328 miles carrying the commander to 40 different cities. In the spring of 1972, the miscellaneous command ship *La Salle* (AGF 3) relieved *Valcour* as flagship for the Middle East Force. Painted white like her forbears, "The Great White Ghost of the Arabian Coast" steamed an average of 55,000 miles annually calling on ports in Africa, Asia, and the Middle East. She served as the MEF flagship until 1993.

The Navy recognized that it not only needed to manage tanker traffic in the Arabian Gulf, but also might need to conduct combat operations to defend America's interests there. In March 1948, *Valley Forge* (CV 45) transited the Strait of Hormuz, becoming the first American aircraft carrier to operate in the Arabian Gulf. *Valley Forge* and other ships conducted extensive reconnaissance and scientific surveys, which indicated that shallow water, extreme heat and humidity, blowing sand, and other environmental conditions in the gulf posed significant operational problems. The carrier's visit included a port call to Ras Tanura, Saudi Arabia. Naval officers and enlisted men enjoyed Arab hospitality, while the show of naval strength impressed Arab leaders. Two months

Arabian Gulf Region.

Sheikh Isa bin Salman al-Khalifa, ruler of Bahrain, departs the flagship Valcour *(AGF 1) after an official visit to Rear Admiral Earl R. Eastwood, Commander Middle East Force, 5 April 1967.*

U.S. Naval Historical Center

Arabian guests, crewmen, and others observe flight operations from Valley Forge's *island structure, 25 March 1948.*

U.S. Naval Historical Center

later, the escort carrier *Rendova* (CVE 114) and destroyer *Charles H. Roan* (DD 853) entered the gulf. The carrier paid a 52-hour visit to Bahrain, the highlight of which was a dinner for 120 guests, including 45 U.S. naval officers, hosted by Sheikh Salman bin Hamad al-Khalifa, Bahrain's ruler. Various U.S. fleet units visited the region periodically throughout the next four decades.

American diplomacy and deployment of large fleet units played a major role in preventing a protracted war across the region that otherwise might have arisen from crises like Iran's nationalization of Western oil fields in the early 1950s, the Suez Crisis of 1956, the Iraq coup of 1958, and the Lebanon intervention of 1958. Although no shots were

fired, such crises often had a direct and sometimes hair-raising impact on American naval forces. In 1963, MEF destroyers deployed to the Red Sea when friction developed between Saudi Arabia and Egypt over civil strife in Yemen. In an "extremely provocative gesture," as the MEF command history put it, Egyptian fighters and bombers with open bomb bay doors flew over the carrier *Essex* (CV 9) as she transited the Suez Canal. In April and May 1967, MEF ships helped evacuate American citizens from Yemen and patrolled off troubled Aden.

The Navy's presence during difficult times demonstrated its permanence in the region and reaffirmed America's intention to defend its allies and interests in the Middle East. +++

CREATION OF
CENTRAL COMMAND AND NAVCENT

D URING THE 1970S AND EARLY 1980s, the United States supplanted Great Britain as the predominant Western power in the Arabian Gulf and Arabian Sea. At the same time, threats to peace and stability in the region skyrocketed. As the danger increased, so did America's commitment to the region's security. This commitment culminated in 1983 in the establishment of a new unified command, U.S. Central Command (CENTCOM), and its naval component, Naval Forces Central Command (NAVCENT).

In January 1968, British Prime Minister Harold Wilson announced that Great Britain would end its defense commitments "east of Suez" and would withdraw its forces from the Arabian Gulf by 1971. The British government conceived the withdrawal as a money-saving measure. In effect, it swept away the last vestiges of the British Empire in the Middle East.

Bahrain had been a British protectorate since 1880, when the British government assumed responsibility for the island's defense. On 14 August 1971, Sheikh Isa bin Salman al-Khalifa declared Bahrain's independence and signed a new treaty of friendship with Britain the next day. Through an agreement with the Bahraini government, the U.S. Navy took over part of the former British naval base at Juffair, naming the facility Administrative Support Unit Bahrain.

The British withdrawal created a great power vacuum in the Arabian Gulf, once considered a British "lake." Determined to fill the void in the region, the Soviets sent a task force into the Indian Ocean and launched diplomatic initiatives to secure permanent bases in countries in and around the gulf. The Soviet navy maintained a continuous presence in the Indian Ocean throughout the 1970s.

The United States was in no position to counter the Soviet moves. With America engaged in the Vietnam War and President Richard M. Nixon committed to extricating U.S. forces from Southeast Asia, the administration sought to avoid new commitments. In 1969, the President annunciated a strategy dubbed the Nixon Doctrine, which envisioned transferring many security responsibilities to regional U.S. allies. In the Arabian Gulf, the Nixon Doctrine resulted in the so-called Twin Pillars policy, which depended upon Iran and Saudi Arabia to provide security for the region and to constitute a bulwark against Soviet expansion there. As a result, American military assistance flowed to Iran and Saudi Arabia for most of the 1970s.

The Twin Pillars policy dovetailed neatly with the plans of Muhammad Reza Pahlavi, the

Two RH-53 Sea Stallions from the carrier Nimitz *(CVN 68) participate in the ill-fated mission to rescue American hostages in Iran, 24 April 1980. Operational difficulties underscored the need to improve how the armed forces worked together.*

U.S. Navy

Somalian Brigadier General Mohammed Hashi Gani welcomes Lieutenant General Robert C. Kingston, commander of the Rapid Deployment Joint Task Force, as he arrives to participate in Exercise Bright Star '82, 1 November 1981.

Shah of Iran, who sought to make his country the preeminent power in the gulf. Emboldened by the surge in oil prices during the mid-1970s and the flood of arms from the United States, the Shah plunged Iran into a pell-mell national modernization program that resulted in waste, inflation, and widespread corruption.

Disgusted with the Shah's seeming disregard for traditional social and religious values, Iranians from all walks of life turned against him and his pro-American government. In 1978, labor strikes, street demonstrations, and riots spread across Iran with increasing frequency and violence. A revolution coalesced around fundamentalist Iranians led by the Ayatollah Ruhollah Khomeini. The Shah went into exile on 16 January 1979. He first went to Egypt, then to Morocco, the Bahamas, Mexico, the United States, Panama, and then back to Egypt, where he died on 27 July 1980 of non-Hodgkin's lymphoma. Soon after the Shah left Iran, Khomeini entered Tehran in triumph and established an anti-Western Islamic theocracy. He and his followers expressed the desire to spread Shiite extremism throughout the Arabian Gulf and expunge Western influence from the region. The Iranian revolutionaries harbored a particularly deep hatred for the United States because Washington had been the Shah's leading supporter. On 4 November 1979 Iranian zealots seized the U.S. Embassy in Tehran and took its staff hostage, marking the beginning of a 444-day crisis.

The situation in the region worsened that December when Soviet forces invaded Afghanistan in support of indigenous communists. Not since World War II had Moscow carried out a military action on this scale. U.S. leaders feared that the Soviets hoped to capitalize on the American-Iranian crisis to secure a warm-water port on the Indian Ocean and to gain control of Arabian Gulf oil resources.

The Soviet invasion of Afghanistan, following hard on the heels of the Iranian revolution, convinced American leaders to take a firm stand in the Arabian Gulf. "Let our position be absolutely clear," President Jimmy Carter declared before Congress on 23 January 1980. "An attempt by any outside force to gain control of the Gulf region will be regarded as an assault on the vital interests of the United States of America, and such an assault will be repelled by any means necessary, including military force." This policy, dubbed the Carter Doctrine, committed American military forces to the defense of the region.

This new policy, inspired by the threats to the Arabian Gulf from the Iranian revolution and the Soviet occupation of Afghanistan, spurred President Carter to create the Rapid Deployment Joint Task Force (RDJTF). Established on 1 March 1980, the RDJTF was a component of what was then called U.S. Readiness Command, and its mission was to rush to the gulf area in the event of a military crisis. The first commander, Marine Lieutenant General P. X. Kelley, was hampered by a lack of bases and forward-positioned equipment, as well as the long distance from the theater. He also didn't "own" any forces and in a crisis would have to "borrow" them from other commands on short notice.

Defense officials in President Ronald Reagan's administration considered the rapid deployment force a poor solution. Accordingly, on 1 January 1983, the Department of Defense replaced the task force with a new unified command: U.S. Central Command, headquartered at MacDill Air Force Base near Tampa, Florida. Initially, its area of

responsibility (AOR) comprised 19 countries, the Red Sea, and the Arabian Gulf, and its mission was to protect free trade, help defend friendly nations, and preserve regional stability. CENTCOM eventually got its own assigned component forces and a four-star commander, putting it on an even footing with European Command, Pacific Command, and Southern Command.

The original 19 countries in Central Command's AOR included Egypt and Sudan in northeast Africa; Djibouti, Ethiopia, Kenya, and Somalia on or near the Horn of Africa; the Yemen Arab Republic, the People's Democratic Republic of Yemen, and the Gulf Cooperation Council (GCC) states of Bahrain, Kuwait, Oman, Qatar, Saudi Arabia, and the United Arab Emirates (UAE) on the Arabian Peninsula; and Jordan, Iraq, Iran, Afghanistan, and Pakistan on the Middle Eastern and South Asian mainland.

By 2005, changes to the Unified Command Plan, which governed the organization of operational

Bradley fighting vehicles parked on the pier beside the fast sealift ship USNS Antares *(T-AKR 294) at Savannah, Georgia, during Exercise Bright Star '97. The capability to deploy combat-ready forces quickly across vast ocean distances enables Central Command to exist.*

Aerial view of the Indian Ocean island of Diego Garcia, 9 December 1998. Naval Station Diego Garcia serves Central Command as a vital air hub, logistics hub, and base for Maritime Prepositioning Squadron Two.

joint forces, had expanded the AOR to 27 countries. On 22 May 1990, the Yemen Arab Republic united with the People's Democratic Republic of Yemen and became the Republic of Yemen. Eritrea came under Central Command's purview after the country gained independence from Ethiopia on 27 April 1993. Because of its cultural and political similarities to the East African mainland, the island nation of Seychelles was added to the AOR on 1 January 1996. Because of their proximity to and political interaction with Iran, Afghanistan, and Pakistan, the five former Soviet Central Asian republics of Kazakhstan, Kyrgyzstan, Tajikistan, Turkmenistan, and Uzbekistan became part of Central Command's AOR on 1 October 1999. On 10 March 2004, Syria and Lebanon were shifted from European Command's jurisdiction to Central Command's jurisdiction because of American concern about Syrian-based terrorists operating in Iraq.

CENTCOM's naval component commander was designated Commander U.S. Naval Forces Central Command (COMUSNAVCENT).

Commander Middle East Force, who had reported to the Commander in Chief, U.S. Naval Forces Europe during the 1970s, was reassigned under Commander in Chief, Central Command (CINCCENT).

The new unified command faced enormous difficulties. None of the countries in the Arabian Gulf region allowed the United States to base ground forces or land-based air forces permanently on their soil. U.S. military leaders knew they would have to deploy sizable, combat-ready forces to the Arabian Gulf region fast enough to cope with an emergency. The problem was how to do so.

The solution they chose was "maritime prepositioning," a concept that had emerged during the Vietnam War. In this approach, the Defense Department maintained equipment, supplies, and vehicles on board Military Sealift Command (MSC) ships that served as floating depots in forward areas. In an emergency, these ships would steam as close as possible to the crisis spot and unload their cargo, even at ports with only rudimentary facilities. Meanwhile, long-range transport aircraft of the Air Force's Military Airlift Command would fly troops to an airfield near the ports where they would "marry up" with their equipment. Planners envisioned a virtual bridge of ships and airplanes to deploy strong forces to the theater and keep them supplied.

The Navy invested $7 billion in strategic sealift programs during the 1980s to make maritime prepositioning a reality. Thirteen specialized roll-on/roll-off prepositioning ships were built or converted from existing hulls. These ships were divided into three maritime prepositioning ship squadrons (MPSRONs) based in the Azores in the eastern Atlantic (MPSRON-1), Diego Garcia (MPSRON-2), and Guam (MPSRON-3). Each squadron contained the equipment and 30 days' worth of supplies for a Marine Expeditionary Brigade (MEB) of 16,500 men. The Army, Air Force, Navy, and Defense Logistics Agency stowed materiel in 11 other prepositioning ships based at Diego Garcia.

In addition, the Defense Department converted eight Sea-Land Corporation container ships (SL-7 class) into fast sealift ships (FSS) capable of making 30 knots and able to load and unload cargo quickly at unimproved ports. These ships were intended to embark a full U.S. Army mechanized division at East Coast ports, transport the unit to a global hot spot, and return to the United States for follow-on ground forces. Moreover, the Department of Transportation followed Navy Department recommendations and expanded its Ready Reserve Force fleet from 36 to 96 cargo ships, tankers, and other auxiliaries.

To improve coordination among the Military Sealift Command, Military Airlift Command, and the Army's Military Traffic Management Command, the Defense Department in 1987 created the joint U.S. Transportation Command, headquartered at Scott Air Force Base, Illinois. These measures went far to ensure swift deployment of combat-ready forces to Southwest Asia.

Although Central Command was responsible for the Arabian Gulf, the Navy's leadership viewed

the region as an extension of the Pacific Basin. The Indian Ocean, Arabian Sea, Gulf of Aden, and Gulf of Oman had long fallen within Pacific Command's area of responsibility, and remained so throughout the 1980s. On 30 December 1983, the Joint Chiefs of Staff (JCS) directed CINCCENT to coordinate with Commander in Chief, Pacific Command (CINCPAC) for contingency plans to integrate the Middle East Force into Pacific Command's Indian Ocean battle force, Task Force 70, during certain crises. For the rest of the 1980s, the Middle East Force flagship remained home-ported in Bahrain, while COMUSNAVCENT headquarters stood in Pearl Harbor, Hawaii.

PH3 Aaron Pineda

A U.S. Marine guides a light armored vehicle down the ramp of the container and roll-on/roll-off ship M/V Cpl. Louis J. Hauge Jr. *during the buildup for Operation Iraqi Freedom, 16 January 2003. This ship had served with Maritime Prepositioning Squadron Two since 1984.*

By the late 1980s, the United States had committed itself to the defense of the Arabian Gulf region, created a unified command to carry out the mission, and invested heavily in programs to ensure its success. The entire commitment hinged upon the Navy's ability to control the sea. Events soon tested the structure and capabilities of the new unified command and its naval component, as well as the very sincerity of America's commitment. +++

THE TANKER WAR

WHILE THE UNITED STATES REORGANIZED its security structure in the Arabian Gulf, the situation in the region grew considerably darker. On 22 September 1980, Iraq launched an offensive into western Iran, marking the beginning of a war that dragged on for eight years and cost the two countries a million dead and a trillion dollars. Although fought mostly on land, the war also included maritime operations, with each side attacking merchant shipping in the Arabian Gulf. In what became known as the Tanker War, between 1980 and 1988 the protagonists attacked hundreds of vessels, killing more than 400 mariners and inflicting losses in the tens of millions of dollars on ship owners, charterers, and insurers. When the Tanker War escalated to the point of threatening free trade in the Arabian Gulf, the Navy stepped in to defend America's interests and allies and to keep the sea lanes open.

Rooted in ancient Sunni-versus-Shia and Arab-versus-Persian religious and ethnic strife and fueled by twentieth-century border disputes, the Iran-Iraq War has been called the "great war of the third world." Iraqi dictator Saddam Hussein claimed to have launched the invasion because of a dispute over the Shatt-al-Arab, the waterway that forms the boundary between Iran and Iraq and empties into the Arabian Gulf.

His real reasons, however, stemmed from delusions of grandeur, a paranoid sense of vulnerability, and a bad politico-military assessment of his eastern neighbor. Saddam sought to consolidate his rising power in the Arab world, to replace Iran as the dominant state in the Arabian Gulf region, and eventually to become a global figure like his hero, Joseph Stalin. Saddam believed that Arab Shiites in southwestern Iran would welcome the invasion as liberation from Persian oppression, and he hoped to grab the western Iranian province of Khuzestan, which contained the bulk of Iran's oil industry.

At the same time, Saddam perceived Iran's fundamentalist agenda as a threat to the vision of revolutionary pan-Arabism articulated by the Baath Arab Socialist Party. The Baath Party was a secular Arab nationalist political party and movement that had arisen in Syria in the 1930s. Saddam had

joined the party as a teenager, Baathists had seized power in Iraq in a July 1968 coup, and Saddam had become leader of the party and head of state in 1979. He maintained power by turning Iraq into a police state and torturing and murdering political opponents and Iraqi citizens who displeased him.

Despite making significant strides in forging an Iraqi nation-state, Saddam feared that Iran's new leadership would threaten Iraq's delicate Sunni-Shia balance and exploit its geo-strategic vulnerabilities, particularly its minimal access to the Arabian Gulf. Finally, Saddam figured Iran would be easy prey, believing that Khomeini's purges of Iran's army and air force had fatally weakened their military capabilities.

As it was, the invasion bogged down quickly. Iraq's air force proved incapable of putting ordnance on target with any sort of accuracy or reliability, while Iraqi ground force tactics proved incapable of overcoming resistance even by lightly armed defenders with any sort of alacrity. As a result, the war degenerated into a stalemate featuring trench lines, human wave assaults, chemical attacks, and massive artillery bombardments reminiscent of World War I. As casualties mounted, Iranian strategy shifted from repelling Saddam's invasion to toppling his regime.

The guided missile frigate Stark *(FFG 31) lists to port after being struck by two Iraqi-launched Exocet missiles on 17 May 1987.*

Now fighting for his life, Saddam turned seaward. For the first three years of the war, attacks on shipping in the Arabian Gulf had been sporadic and generally uncoordinated, with 48 vessels coming under fire. Because oil and the control of its export constituted the lifeblood of both sides, control of merchant shipping routes, destruction of enemy and enemy allied merchant ships, and protection of oil export assets became key objectives in Iraq's strategy and operations. By 1984, the Iraqi air force's growing proficiency at hitting targets enabled Baghdad to escalate operations against Iranian oil facilities and tankers. Thus began the second phase of the Iran-Iraq War's so-called Tanker War. Iraq hoped to weaken Iran's economy by reducing its oil-export capacity, to internationalize the war in an attempt to gain foreign support, to reduce pressure on its ground forces, and to bring Iran to the negotiating table.

Before 1984, Iran remained content to accept maritime losses while seeking victory on land. But

Iraq's escalation of antishipping operations besieged Iran's economy and precipitated a change in Iran's maritime strategy. Iran's leaders realized that with the exception of Iraq's old rivals, Syria and Libya, most of the Arab world was providing financial and military aid to Saddam. Since Iraq possessed few of its own maritime assets worth attacking, Iran responded in kind to Iraq's maritime onslaught by targeting ships trading with Iraq's gulf allies. Seventy-one merchant ships were attacked in 1984 alone, compared with 48 in the first three years of the war.

In March 1984, Iraq initiated sustained naval operations in a self-declared 1,126-kilometer maritime exclusion zone, extending from the mouth of the Shatt-al-Arab to Iran's port of Bushehr. The intensity of the maritime part of the Iran-Iraq War waxed and waned over the ensuing months.

In 1986, Iraq stepped up its air raids on tankers serving Iran and Iranian oil-exporting facilities. Iran responded by escalating its attacks, using aircraft,

Crewmembers stand watch at a 50-caliber machine-gun station on board the amphibious ship Okinawa *(LPH 3) during Operation Earnest Will, 1 November 1987.*

speedboats, sea mines, and land-based Silkworm antiship missiles, against tankers serving Arab ports in the gulf. Because Kuwait was devoting a significant proportion of its oil revenues to support Iraq's war effort, the Iranians focused heavily on Kuwaiti tankers and merchant ships trading with Kuwait. That fall, the Kuwaiti government began seeking help from the international community in dealing with the Iranian onslaught.

On 13 January 1987, the Emir's government asked the U.S. government permission for Kuwaiti tankers to fly the American flag in the gulf, thereby enabling them to receive the same protection as merchantmen under American registry. The Kuwaitis figured that American naval protection would deter or defeat Iranian aggression against the reflagged tankers. The Kuwait government had already made similar inquiries to the governments of the United Kingdom, China, and the Soviet Union, and Britain had already begun reflagging ships.

From the U.S. perspective, the Iran-Iraq War posed a difficult dilemma. While the land war made little immediate impact beyond Iranian and Iraqi territory, strikes on shore-based oil production and export facilities, offshore platforms, and tankers created a ripple effect that reached around the world. Although the United States was not dependent on gulf oil, its allies were. America imported less than 10 percent of its oil from the region during the mid-1980s, but Western Europe imported approximately 30 percent and Japan approximately 60 percent of their oil from gulf states. By 1986, the Tanker War had significantly reduced shipping in the gulf and had caused insurance rates on tankers to skyrocket. Worse still, the fighting impeded the flow of gulf oil to the rest of the world and had the potential to damage the global economy. U.S. leaders were also alarmed by the prospect of an Iranian victory and its potential to spread Shiite fundamentalism throughout the region and to destabilize America's gulf allies.

But it was the specter of the Soviets using the escort mission to project power into the region that finally precipitated U.S. government action. Arabian Gulf sea lanes, declared President Reagan, "will not be allowed to come under the control of the Soviet Union." On 7 March 1987, the United States government announced its decision to authorize 11 Kuwaiti tankers to sail under U.S. registry. The two governments signed a reflagging agreement on 2 April.

The governments of Great Britain, France, Italy, Belgium, and Netherlands likewise grasped the importance of preventing Iranian depredations to oceangoing commerce and maintaining freedom of the seas, so they too dispatched ships to the gulf. Bahrain, Kuwait, Saudi Arabia, and the United Arab Emirates contributed fuel to the effort and granted access to gulf port facilities and airbases.

Because American naval leaders remained uncertain about how Iran would respond, the U.S. Navy deployed a substantial task force, the largest of the naval contingents involved in escorting Kuwaiti tankers. By the end of 1987, the Navy had deployed 13 warships inside the gulf to carry out the operation, code-named Earnest Will. A U.S. carrier battle group steaming in the Gulf of Oman increased the Navy's strength in the theater to between 25 and 30 warships and provided the means to strike targets inside Iran, if it became necessary.

The Navy did not, however, consider operating carriers inside the Arabian Gulf. No American aircraft carrier had operated extensively inside the Strait of Hormuz since *Constellation* (CV 64) took part in Midlink 74, the largest naval exercise held in the Arabian Sea to that point. Throughout the 1980s, naval leaders believed that the benefits of operating carriers inside the gulf were not worth the risks posed by uncharted hazards, a perceived lack of sufficient deep water to conduct flight operations, and Iranian mines and antiship missiles. Aircraft carriers were kept in the deeper and less threatening Arabian Sea, despite being hundreds of miles farther away from potential targets.

A line of reflagged Kuwaiti tankers steams through the gulf under U.S. Navy escort, 1 September 1987.

A lookout scans the horizon from the bridge of the cruiser Fox (CG 33), *escorting the reflagged Kuwaiti supertankers* Gas Prince *and* Bridgeton, *21 July 1987.*

The Navy's unwillingness to operate carriers inside the gulf exacerbated command and control problems that arose during Earnest Will. Part of the difficulty lay in the fact that the operation unfolded on the boundary of two unified commands. The Middle East Force operated inside the Arabian Gulf under CINCCENT, while the carrier group steaming in the Gulf of Oman operated under CINCPAC. Navy leaders involved in planning the operation wanted a Pacific Fleet admiral to command the naval forces operating in Central Command's area of responsibility. The fact that the commander in chief of Central Command was a Marine—General George B. Crist—perturbed naval leaders who believed that only one of their own had the training necessary to lead naval operations. The Chief of Naval Operations even proposed reassigning the Red Sea and Arabian Gulf from CINCCENT to CINCPAC. The Joint Chiefs of Staff declined.

Technically, Central Command's naval component commander should have led the naval forces in the theater, particularly in the wake of the passage of the Goldwater-Nichols Department of Defense Reorganization Act of 1986. Confused command relationships, incompatible communications, inadequate intelligence sharing, and different service approaches to tactical problems had hampered joint operations during the failed Iran hostage rescue mission of 1980, the peacekeeping mission in Lebanon of 1982–1984, and the Grenada intervention of 1983. Goldwater-Nichols sought to resolve these problems. It increased the power of the JCS chairman, the Joint Staff, and the commanders in chief of the combatant commands while reducing the power of the service chiefs.

From the Navy's perspective, however, this emphasis on "jointness" came at the expense of the service's traditional independence. Naval officers considered service on a joint staff detrimental to one's career. The Navy even had developed its own strategy, the Maritime Strategy, publicly articulated in January 1986, which it used to justify its force structure.

Pacific Fleet's claims to the Indian Ocean area and the Navy's resistance to jointness made the service reluctant to subordinate forces to Central Command. In 1987 COMUSNAVCENT was Rear Admiral (Select) Philip F. Duffy, who, in practice, managed only the logistic and administrative support of naval forces in the gulf. Although the Navy had close ties to countries in the region, CINCCENT's requests that the Navy assign a more senior officer to the NAVCENT billet made no headway in the Office of the Chief of Naval Operations (OPNAV).

Nevertheless, General Crist persuaded Admiral William J. Crowe, the chairman of the Joint Chiefs of Staff, that CINCCENT needed to have sole control of naval operations in the theater. They arranged a compromise with OPNAV. On 20 September 1987, the Department of Defense established the Joint Task Force Middle East (JTFME), a temporary command and control organization tailored specifically to fit the needs of Operation Earnest Will. Owing to the predominantly maritime nature of the mission, and "to satisfy the Navy's sensibilities," as Admiral Crowe put it, Rear Admiral Dennis M. Brooks, flying his flag with the carrier battle group in the North Arabian Sea, was designated Commander JTFME. Brooks answered to Crist for operational direction.

Iranian ship Iran Ajr, *captured while laying mines off the coast of Bahrain, with a U.S. Navy landing craft alongside, 22 September 1987.*

The destroyer John Young *(DD 973) shells a pair of Iranian command and control platforms in response to an Iranian attack on a reflagged Kuwaiti tanker, 19 October 1987.*

The command structure still did not function smoothly because Commander Middle East Force, Rear Admiral Harold J. Bernsen, retained a degree of autonomy, and he and Brooks clashed repeatedly. To resolve this problem, Crowe combined JTFME and the MEF under Brooks' successor, Rear Admiral Anthony Less.

U.S. naval forces operating in the gulf faced operational as well as organizational difficulties. On 17 May 1987, an Iraqi Mirage F-1 pilot mistook the U.S. frigate *Stark* (FFG 31) for an Iranian vessel and struck her with two Exocet air-to-surface missiles. The night attack killed 37 American Sailors, but their surviving shipmates saved *Stark* from sinking with a dogged and skillful damage control effort.

On 24 July, during the U.S. Navy's first Earnest Will convoy escort mission, an Iranian-laid sea mine damaged the reflagged tanker *Bridgeton*. The Navy's mine countermeasures forces in the area, consisting of eight MH-53 helicopters and a small flotilla of ocean minesweepers, found and destroyed numerous mines during these and later operations in the gulf. Nonetheless, the aircraft were too few and the minesweepers too old, having seen almost forty years of hard service, to accomplish the clearance mission adequately. American naval leaders hoped to compensate for this deficiency by employing a traditional mine warfare tactic—preventing the enemy from laying the weapons. In that regard, American forces in the gulf scored a major success on 21 September, when U.S. Army AH-6 Seabat helicopters, operating from the deck of guided missile frigate *Jarrett* (FFG 33), intercepted the Iranian vessel *Iran Ajr* in the act of dropping mines into the water. In a swift action, the joint team captured the minelayer. That October, the joint frigate-Seabat team sank a speedboat and captured two others when the Iranians opened fire on the aircraft.

Undeterred, the Iranians struck and damaged the reflagged tanker *Sea Isle City* with a Chinese-supplied Silkworm missile. In retaliation, the Navy destroyed two Iranian oil platforms being used as military outposts. On 14 April 1988, guided missile frigate *Samuel B. Roberts* (FFG 58) struck an Iranian mine that blew a 22-foot hole in her side and wounded ten Sailors.

To drive home the point that the United States would not tolerate such attacks and remained determined to protect its allies and interests in the gulf, the Navy launched against Iranian forces another retaliatory strike, code-named Operation Praying Mantis. On 18 April, surface ships and carrier-based aircraft destroyed two gulf oil platforms used by the Iranian military. In this battle, U.S. naval forces sank or damaged half of Iran's operational navy. Even though a few Iranian fast attack craft continued to fire on American warships and merchantmen, Praying Mantis greatly reduced the threat to shipping.

Then, on 3 July, guided missile cruiser *Vincennes* (CG 49) mistook an Iranian airliner for an attacking warplane and shot it down, killing 290 passengers and crew. This sad episode seemed to be the last straw for the Iranian people, reeling from almost a decade of revolution and war. Tehran's ground forces tottered on the brink of collapse under the weight of an Iraqi offensive. Antiwar demonstrations had broken out in Isfahan and Tabriz. The economy was in ruins, the treasury bankrupt. On 18 July, the Iranians agreed to accept a U.N. cease-fire proposal. The war with Iraq, and with it the Tanker War, soon came to an end.

Operation Earnest Will had succeeded, and the Navy's ships, aircraft, weapons, and personnel generally performed well in conducting littoral operations. But problems had arisen in two areas—mine warfare and command and control. Naval leaders recognized that the mine countermeasures force needed modernization and took steps to acquire new ships and equipment. They were less inclined to explore new approaches to melding theater and naval operations. If anything, naval leaders ascribed the difficulties that Commander JTFME experienced with command and control of operations in the gulf to outside interference.

Despite these difficulties, the U.S. Navy-led Joint Task Force Middle East, working with America's European and Arabian Gulf allies, accomplished the mission of protecting the vital gulf tanker traffic. Earnest Will had also taken some of the sting from Iran's revolutionary movement. Finally, the United States' stand in the gulf during 1987–1988 erased the negative images resulting from the failed Iranian rescue mission and withdrawal from Lebanon, persuading the region's leaders that they could count on the United States.

Lieutenant Dan Taylor climbs down from the frigate Nicholas *(FFG 47) into a motor whaleboat for transfer to a reflagged Kuwaiti tanker, where he will serve as liaison officer during a tanker escort mission, 1 July 1988.*

Meanwhile, relative quiet returned to the Arabian Gulf. The United States gradually reduced its forces in the region. By the summer of 1990, only five naval vessels patrolled the gulf, the smallest contingent since the late 1970s. +++

DESERT SHIELD AND DESERT STORM

THE QUIET DIDN'T LAST LONG. Saddam Hussein's megalomaniacal dream of becoming the Stalin of the Middle East survived the war with Iran, despite the war's exorbitant cost to Iraq in blood and treasure. This time, however, the dictator sought to satisfy his lust for conquest by choosing what he thought would be a much easier target. On 2 August 1990, Iraqi Republican Guard armored and mechanized units rolled into Kuwait. Six days later, Saddam announced the annexation of Kuwait, declaring it Iraq's nineteenth province. Saddam figured nobody—not Arab nations, the United Nations, or the United States—would contest the invasion. He believed America possessed neither the will nor the ability to go to war in Southwest Asia. It was another bad politico-military assessment. Within seven months, the United States had taken the lead in an international coalition that had prevented further Iraqi conquests and had driven Saddam's forces out of Kuwait. The Navy's ability to control the sea and project power ashore proved critical to the success of Desert Shield, while its warfighting capabilities played a key role in the coalition's victory over Iraq during Desert Storm.

American naval forces responded immediately to Iraq's invasion of Kuwait. Within an hour, the *Independence* (CV 62) carrier battle group, cruising in the Indian Ocean near Diego Garcia, headed for the Gulf of Oman, while the *Dwight D. Eisenhower* (CVN 69) carrier battle group, nearing the end of a deployment to the central Mediterranean, set a course for the Red Sea. Within three days carrier-borne aircraft had come within striking distance of Saddam's tank columns.

On 4 August, President George H.W. Bush decided that military power offered the best hope of deterring or halting further Iraqi aggression. On 6 August, at the invitation of Saudi King Abdul Aziz Ibn Fahd, the President ordered American forces to Saudi Arabia.

Central Command's Operation Plan (OPLAN) 1002-90, the latest in a series of U.S. war plans for defense of the gulf region, guided the deployment. With the end of the Cold War in 1989, the resultant shift in U.S. strategic focus from global war to regional conflict, and the emergence of Iraq as the preeminent military power in the gulf, Department of Defense and CENTCOM planners had based 1002-90 on a scenario involving a potential Iraqi attack down the Arabian Peninsula. The plan called for the deployment of American naval, air, and ground forces to deter or counterattack an Iraqi invasion of Saudi Arabia.

Operation Desert Shield, as the deployment to Saudi Arabia was called, unfolded in two phases. The first—a defensive phase—lasted through 31 October 1990. The second—preparation for an offensive—lasted from 1 November 1990 to 16 January 1991. The next day Central Command launched Operation Desert Storm to push Iraqi forces out of Kuwait. Together these operations became known as the Gulf War.

Like the Tanker War, command and control of naval operations during the Gulf War proved problematic. Although the Secretary of Defense had tried to resolve Pacific Command's boundary dispute by reassigning the Gulfs of Aden and Oman to CENTCOM's area of responsibility on

IRAN

IRAQ

Al Basrah

Persian

Gulf

Būbiyān

Kuwait

Kuwait Bay

Al Jahrā'

Al Aḥmadī

Ar Rawḍatayn

Kuwait

Kuwait

— International boundary
★ National capital
— Railroad
— Expressway
— Road
Built-up area

0   10   20   30 Kilometers

0   10   20   30 Miles

SAUDI ARABIA

Al Khabal

Kuwait.

26 June 1989, nothing had changed in the Navy's organization or attitude with regard to Central Command. On the eve of the invasion of Kuwait, COMUSNAVCENT, Rear Admiral (Select) Robert Sutton, was still junior to the three-star commanders of Central Command's other service components. For a large-scale operation like Desert Shield, naval leaders still expected Pacific Command to supply an admiral to lead naval operations in support of Central Command, rather than as a component of Central Command. As a result of this attitude, three-star officers from the other services had played major roles in the staff work and exercises to develop OPLAN 1002-90, but the Navy had provided no such input.

The cruiser Bunker Hill (CG 52) launches a Tomahawk land attack missile (TLAM) toward a target in Iraq, January 1991. Operation Desert Storm marked the TLAM's combat debut. The destroyer Paul F. Foster (DD 964) steams at right

Once again, the Department of Defense brokered a compromise. The commander of Pacific Command's Seventh Fleet, Vice Admiral Henry H. Mauz Jr., was designated COMUSNAVCENT under General H. Norman Schwarzkopf Jr., CENTCOM's commander in chief. Sutton remained in Hawaii under the title COMUSNAVCENT Pearl Harbor and retained responsibility for sealift coordination, logistics, and personnel support throughout the Gulf War. Rear Admiral William Fogarty, who had been commander of Joint Task Force Middle East on the eve of the Iraqi invasion, became Commander Middle East Force. While the other component commanders established forward headquarters at Riyadh, Saudi Arabia, with General Schwarzkopf, Admiral Mauz decided to exercise command from the Seventh Fleet flagship Blue Ridge (LCC 19).

Admiral Mauz assigned relatively junior naval officers to joint duties within Central Command. For liaison duty with CENTCOM headquarters, he created the billet of NAVCENT Riyadh, to which he appointed Rear Admiral Timothy W. Wright. For liaison duty with Air Force Lieutenant General Charles Horner, the Air Force component commander and Joint Force Air Component Commander (JFACC), Admiral Mauz assigned a group of officers designated the Fleet Coordinating Group and led by a Navy captain. Although these command arrangements reflected the Navy's tradition of independence, the commitment of relatively junior officers to CENTCOM's joint team and the lack of a prominent role in prewar joint planning and exercising strained NAVCENT's relationships with the other components and added undue difficulties to the conduct of joint operations, particularly in adjusting to the air component commander's Air Tasking Order (ATO) system of flight operations management. The fact that the daily ATO itself had to be flown out to the carriers instead of transmitted electronically symbolized the Navy's joint organizational and operational problems during Desert Shield and Desert Storm.

Fortunately, these problems created only minor bumps on the road to victory. American forces began arriving in Saudi Arabia on 7 August. In general, Soldiers, Marines, Airmen, and Navy Reservists reached the theater by air, while more than 90 percent of their equipment and supplies came by sea.

From mid-August to early September, naval forces afloat and ashore made up the bulk of allied military power facing Saddam Hussein. On 15 August, the first three ships of Maritime Prepositioning Ship Squadron Two reached the Saudi port of Jubayl. MPSRON-2 carried the equipment and 30 days of supplies for the 7th Marine Expeditionary Brigade. The Marines, who had begun to arrive at Jubayl's air facilities on the 14th, "married up" with their ship-delivered equipment and stood ready for combat 11 days later. By 1 September, U.S. naval forces in the Arabian Gulf, North Arabian Sea, and Red Sea included three carriers, one battleship, six cruisers, five destroyers, and eight frigates.

Allied nations also deployed ships and aircraft to oppose Iraq's aggression. Eventually, naval forces from Argentina, Australia, Belgium, Canada, Denmark, France, Germany, Greece, Italy, Kuwait, the Netherlands, Norway, Poland, Portugal, Spain, the Soviet Union, and the United Kingdom participated in one way or another in Desert Shield, Desert Storm, and the aftermath of the war.

Admiral Mauz soon realized he would have to operate carriers in the Arabian Gulf if the Navy were to contribute effectively to the war. Successful late Cold War experiments to place carriers in confined waters like those surrounding the Norwegian fjords and the Aleutian, Aegean, and Japanese islands suggested that aircraft carriers could, in fact, conduct safe operations in shallow waters close to land. By Mauz's order, the *Independence* battle group transited the Strait of Hormuz on 2 October and proved that flight operations were feasible in the gulf. From then on, the question was not whether carriers could operate in the gulf, but how many.

During the first phase of Desert Shield, ships operated by Military Sealift Command delivered 1,034,900 tons of equipment, 135,100 tons of supplies, and 1,800,000 tons of petroleum products to the Arabian Gulf region. Of the 173 ships involved, 124 were U.S.-flag vessels, and these

accounted for 85 percent of the tonnage. Even though Phase I ended formally on 5 December, virtually all of CENTCOM's planned requirements had been satisfied by 11 November. At the same time, the United States deployed more than 60 naval vessels, 1,000 ground-based aircraft, and 240,000 military men and women to the theater. On 1 November General Colin Powell, chairman of the Joint Chiefs of Staff, reported to the President that General Schwarzkopf "had the combat capability in place, in the region, to successfully defend against any Iraqi attack."

Saddam's negative responses to U.N. political initiatives during the fall of 1990 made it increasingly clear that an offensive operation would be necessary

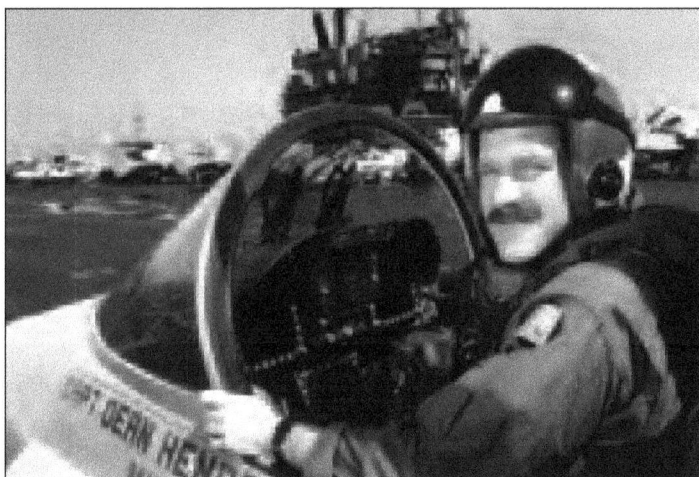

Lieutenant Commander Mark Fox, the first coalition pilot to shoot down an Iraqi MiG, in the cockpit of the F/A-18C Hornet he flew during the mission.

to drive Iraqi forces from Kuwait. In August, Air Force and CENTCOM planners worked up the first draft of a plan for a four-phase air, land, and sea campaign to eject Iraqi forces from Kuwait, code-named Desert Storm. On 31 October, President Bush decided to deploy an additional 200,000 Sailors, Soldiers, Airmen, and Marines to the theater.

Most U.S. air and naval forces deployed during Phase II arrived in the theater by mid-January. As in Phase I, people came largely by air and cargo by sea. During Phase II, 220 MSC-controlled ships delivered 1,270,300 short tons of equipment, 235,400 more than in the earlier effort. The 404,700 tons of supplies delivered in Phase II almost

Two A-7 Corsair II jets loaded with cluster bombs and AIM-9 Sidewinder missiles streak toward a target in Iraq, 1 February 1991. The Navy retired its last A-7s in May 1991.

tripled that of Phase I. Finally, MSC delivered to theater forces 3,500,000 short tons of fuel, 1,700,000 more than in Phase I.

While merchantmen delivered supplies and equipment, combatants prepared for war. On 1 December 1990, Vice Admiral Stanley Arthur became COMUSNAVCENT in a routine turnover. Admiral Arthur divided the carrier battle groups into two battle forces, designated Zulu and Yankee, which operated respectively in the Arabian Gulf and Red Sea. Naval air wings rehearsed strike operations at Fallon, Nevada, before departing for the theater. Battle Force Yankee conducted "mirror-image" strike exercises with Air Force units. Other naval units conducted combat search and rescue, surface warfare, antiair warfare, gunfire support, amphibious landing, and a wide variety of other exercises.

Even as coalition forces prepared for war, the allies sought a peaceful exit for the Iraqi army in Kuwait. But after Saddam refused to withdraw, the coalition launched Operation Desert Storm on 17 January 1991.

At that time, Iraq fielded the world's fourth largest army and sixth largest air force. Iraqi ground forces in the Kuwaiti Theater of Operations numbered 43 divisions. Twenty-five of them occupied two major defensive belts along the Kuwaiti-Saudi border. The remaining 18 divisions stood by in reserve, including eight Republican Guard divisions positioned north and west of Kuwait. The Iraqi navy's 165 vessels, including 13 missile boats, were sitting in port or operating along the Kuwaiti coast. Iraq's air force numbered approximately 950 aircraft.

On the coalition side, seven U.S. Army divisions, two Marine Corps divisions, a British armored division, a French light armored division, and the equivalent of four Arab divisions stood ready for action. More than 2,400 fixed-wing aircraft from 12 coalition countries flew from bases and aircraft carriers throughout the theater and around the world. In all, more than 600,000 men and women from 31 nations prepared to liberate Kuwait.

The coalition naval armada numbered more than 150 ships from 14 nations. The United States Navy contributed 108 of these ships, including five carrier battle groups, two battleships, 13 submarines, and the largest amphibious force mustered since the Korean War, carrying nearly 17,000 Marines. The *John F. Kennedy* (CV 67), *Saratoga* (CV 60), and *America* (CV 66) battle groups operated in the Red

Sea while the *Ranger* (CV 61) and *Midway* (CV 41) battle groups steamed in the Arabian Gulf. The *Theodore Roosevelt* (CVN 71) battle group arrived on station in the gulf in January 1991. The *America* battle group rounded the Arabian Peninsula in February, bringing the number of carriers operating in the gulf to four. The naval array also featured special warfare forces, naval construction battalions, medical units, cargo handlers, logistics ships and aircraft, explosive ordnance disposal (EOD) units, mine countermeasures (MCM) ships, salvage and repair units, and harbor defense forces.

CENTCOM's four-phase theater campaign plan for Operation Desert Storm sought to expel the Iraqi army of occupation from Kuwait and to destroy Iraq's offensive capabilities to prevent future aggression. Phase I was a strategic air campaign aimed at rendering Iraqi forces blind, deaf, and immobile, while leaving the basic economic and industrial infrastructure of the country intact. In Phase II, allied forces would establish air superiority in the Kuwaiti Theater of Operations. In Phase III, air and naval power would prepare the battlefield by isolating and reducing enemy forces in the theater. Phases I–III of the theater plan—strategic attack, air supremacy, and battlefield preparation—made up the air campaign. If Saddam refused to capitulate during Phases I–III, the coalition would launch Phase IV, a ground offensive aimed at ejecting the Iraqis from Kuwait.

Naval forces had two primary missions in Desert Storm: support the air campaign and convince Saddam that the allies intended to launch an amphibious assault on his left flank. U.S. leaders had considered making a Navy-Marine amphibious landing in Kuwait or southern Iraq in support of the main ground thrust, but staff studies and simulations run in the fall of 1990 raised the specter of heavy casualties in the face of enemy beach defenses and sea minefields. Therefore, General Schwarzkopf never seriously considered a major

U.S. Marines roll into Kuwait International Airport in light armored vehicles, 27 February 1991.

An Iraqi patrol boat lies dead in the water after a Sea Skua missile attack by a British Lynx helicopter based on the destroyer HMS Gloucester *(D 96).*

weapons struck targets with remarkable accuracy hundreds of miles from the sea in heavily defended Baghdad without risking the life of a single naval aviator. Tomahawks added a new dimension to the traditional Navy mission of projecting power ashore.

In the first few days of Desert Storm, coalition air forces won air superiority and fragmented Saddam's strategic air defenses and command, control, and communications network. For the rest of January the coalition focused the bulk of its air power against strategic targets. On 27 January, Schwarzkopf announced that the coalition had won air supremacy over Iraq and Kuwait. Iraqi air defenses retained the ability to react piecemeal to allied strikes but could no longer coordinate defensive actions.

In the early evening of 29 January 1991, Iraqi armor and mechanized infantry in eastern and southern Kuwait attacked U.S. Marine and Arab coalition units along the Kuwaiti-Saudi Arabian border. At the same time, Iraqi commandos embarked in 15 small patrol boats sortied south along the coast with orders to infiltrate and create havoc in the coalition's rear. Saddam sought to provoke a major ground engagement, hoping to inflict so many casualties on American forces that congressional and public opinion would turn against the war. The Iraqis achieved tactical surprise and occupied the Saudi Arabian oil and resort town of Khafji, whose population had been evacuated long before because the town lay within range of Iraqi artillery in Kuwait.

Coalition fixed-wing and rotary-wing aircraft struck back hard, decimating the attacking Iraqi columns, preventing reinforcement of engaged Iraqi units on land, and sinking or scattering all of the Iraqi patrol boats. By the time the battle ended on 2 February, the coalition had forced elements of two Iraqi divisions to retreat in disarray back to Kuwait,

amphibious landing on the Iraqi-held shore. But rather than disembark the amphibious forces, he used them for deception operations.

The Tomahawk Land Attack Missile (TLAM) made its combat debut during the first wave of coalition attacks. The Tomahawk was a long range cruise missile, launched by surface ships and submarines at targets on land. The missiles flew at low altitudes at high subsonic speeds, guided over evasive routes by different navigation systems. Variants could carry 1,000-pound high-explosive, bomblet-dispensing, nuclear, and other kinds of warheads. Navy surface ships and submarines successfully launched 122 TLAMs on the first day and 282 throughout the course of the war. These destroyed some 600 enemy vehicles, and recovered all lost territory with minimal friendly losses. Khafji was the only major Iraqi offensive of the war and its outcome demonstrated the impotence of Iraq's army in the face of coalition air power.

Although Phase I operations continued throughout the war, by early February the weight of the allied air attack had shifted from strategic targets in Iraq to Phase III targets—Iraqi ground forces—in the Kuwaiti Theater of Operations. From Schwarzkopf's perspective, this phase was intended to soften up enemy ground forces in preparation for Phase IV, the ground offensive. The plan for the final assault envisioned the main attack as a "left hook" by armor-heavy forces wheeling around the enemy right flank, cutting off Iraqi forces in Kuwait, and destroying the Republican Guard. The amphibious deception operations were designed to divert Iraqi attention from the main thrust and to pin Iraqi units to the coast. Supporting attacks by the I Marine Expeditionary Force (MEF) and Arab units along the Kuwaiti-Saudi border would fix and destroy Iraqi forces in Kuwait.

Navy and Marine Corps aviation proved essential to the success of the 43-day air campaign, during which allied air forces flew more than 100,000 sorties at an average of 2,500 sorties per day. The 600 aircraft contributed by the naval services accounted for 28 percent of the coalition's 2,300-plane armada and flew an average of 650 sorties per day.

While naval aviation did its part to dismantle Iraq's war machine, Admiral Arthur carried out his mission of convincing Saddam that the allies intended to launch an amphibious assault on Iraq's left flank. To pull off this deception, Arthur planned a two-stage maritime campaign: establish sea and air control in the northern gulf, and then conduct inshore operations in the northern gulf.

The first stage involved clearing a path to the coast of Kuwait along Saddam's seaward flank. The obstacles included the Iraqi navy and enemy troops posted on oil platforms and islands in the northern gulf. Rear Admiral Ronald J. Zlatoper, Commander Carrier Group Seven and antisurface warfare commander in the gulf, devised an aggressive "rollback" concept to neutralize Iraqi naval vessels

Oil well fires rage outside Kuwait City in the aftermath of Operation Desert Storm, 21 March 1991. Iraqi forces torched the wells before coalition forces drove them from Kuwait.

Jubilant soldiers and civilians wave American, British, Saudi, and Kuwaiti flags after the retreat of Iraqi soldiers from Kuwait City, 27 February 1991.

and troops posted on oil platforms and islands. He aimed not only to defend the fleet from attack but also to seek out and destroy enemy naval forces at sea, along inland waterways, and in port.

From 17 to 20 January, the U.S. guided missile frigate *Nicholas* (FFG 47) and the Kuwaiti guided missile patrol boats *Istiqlal* and *al-Sanbouk* cleared Iraqi forces from the ad-Dorra offshore oil platforms, capturing the war's first enemy prisoners of war in the process. From 22 January through the end of the month, allied aircraft flying offensive antisurface missions engaged Iraqi port facilities, Silkworm missile sites, or naval craft on a daily basis. On 30 January, in what became known as the Battle of Bubiyan Channel, or the Bubiyan "Turkey Shoot," a large force of Iraqi combatants based at Iraq's Az Zubayr and Umm Qasr naval bases sortied on a high-speed dash for Iran. Saddam himself issued the sailing orders, hoping to preserve the boats for the postwar era. Coalition forces detected the movement and attacked the fleeing vessels for the

next 13 hours. In 21 separate engagements, coalition naval aircraft destroyed or damaged seven missile boats, three amphibious ships, a minesweeper, and nine other Iraqi vessels in the shallow waters between Bubiyan Island and the Shatt-al-Arab marshlands. Only one missile boat and one amphibious ship, both shot up, escaped.

By 2 February, coalition forces had destroyed or disabled all 13 enemy missile boats and many other combatants. Although the Navy conducted antisurface missions for the rest of the war, it had eliminated the principal surface threat to the coalition. On 8 February, Admiral Arthur declared that the coalition had established sea control in the northern Arabian Gulf.

The successful offensive antisurface operations made it possible for the second stage of the maritime campaign to begin. In this stage, mine countermeasures forces cleared gunfire support areas and amphibious assault lanes to the Kuwaiti coast. Then, battleships moved in to bombard Iraqi positions ashore while the amphibious task force feigned assaults and conducted raids. Task Group 151.11, consisting of amphibious ship *Tripoli* (LPH 10), battleships *Wisconsin* (BB 64) and *Missouri* (BB 63), 13 U.S., British, and Saudi MCM vessels, and 15 U.S. and British cruisers, destroyers, frigates, and support ships, steamed into the northern gulf on 13 February.

Mine countermeasures operations commenced three days later. U.S. forces consisted of the newly commissioned minehunter *Avenger* (MCM 1), three 40-year-old minesweepers, and six MH-53E helicopters based on *Tripoli*. The Royal Navy deployed five Hunt-class vessels, the most sophisticated minehunter ships in the world.

Since early fall NAVCENT had been receiving reports that the Iraqis were placing mines in Kuwaiti and northern gulf waters. Unfortunately, the Navy could do little to monitor the situation because General Schwarzkopf had prohibited allied aircraft from flying north of 27°45' north latitude and naval forces from steaming north of 27°30' north latitude, fearing that reconnaissance operations closer to occupied Kuwait might trigger a war prematurely. As a result, allied naval forces could only guess at the location of Iraqi minefields. The initial intelligence assessment, based on limited information, led the MCM staff to believe that the minefields lay much closer to the coast than they actually did.

The MCM ships began operations at a point they believed to be outside the Iraqi minefields, but they actually passed through the main minefields before turning on their equipment. Their initial mission was to clear a 15-mile-long, 1,000-yard-wide transit lane and a 10-mile by 3.5-mile fire support area south of Failaka Island, in preparation for an amphibious raid there.

On 18 February, *Tripoli* and the cruiser *Princeton* (CG 59) both struck mines. No one died as a result, but both ships received extensive damage. Nevertheless, the coalition got off relatively lightly in Saddam's minefields. Prior to the mine strikes, several different allied warships had also been operating unknowingly in mined waters. And if *Tripoli* and *Princeton* had not struck mines, the rest of Task Group 151.11 would have steamed westward into mine-infested waters. Fortunately, many of the Iraqi mines had been improperly deployed, rendering many of them ineffective. Nevertheless, the recently discovered minefields led Schwarzkopf to cancel the Failaka Island raid and reinforced his decision not to launch a major amphibious assault.

After leading the rest of Task Group 151.11 east of mined waters, the MCM group resumed channel-clearing operations from a point farther out to sea, beyond the minefields, and worked westward. By the evening of 23 February, the MCM group had cleared a narrow, 1,000–2,000-yard-wide, 31-mile-long swath of water, enabling *Missouri*, the task group's new flagship, to commence bombardment of enemy positions ashore. From 24 to 28 February, MCM forces worked to clear a channel to the Kuwaiti port of Ash Shuaybah.

Despite the fact that Phase III air operations were steadily reducing the combat potential of the Iraqi army, Saddam showed no sign of capitulation. General Schwarzkopf launched the ground offensive on 24 February.

On the eve of the final assault, coalition forces stood along a line stretching 300 miles west from the Arabian Gulf into the desert, arrayed in four major formations. The Army's XVIII Airborne Corps and VII Corps held the westernmost position and would launch the main attack. The Joint Forces Command-North, consisting of Egyptian, Syrian, Saudi, and Kuwaiti forces, occupied the center of the line. To their right stood the I MEF poised to drive into the heart of Kuwait. The Joint Forces Command-East, consisting of units from all six GCC states (Bahrain, Kuwait, Oman, Qatar, Saudi Arabia, and the United Arab Emirates) anchored the coalition line on the coast. Out in the Arabian Gulf, the 4th and 5th Marine Expeditionary Brigades remained embarked in the 31 ships of Amphibious Groups Two and Three, ready to launch or to feign landings as necessary.

At 0800 on 23 February, *Wisconsin* commenced shelling targets in Kuwait just north of the border to support the Joint Forces Command-East, which would begin its attack the next day. *Wisconsin*'s projectiles rained down on Iraqi artillery and infantry positions, ammunition storage facilities, and logistics sites. At 2315, *Missouri* began shelling Failaka Island to create the impression that a full-scale landing was coming in order to freeze Iraqi mobile reserves in position. That same night, SEALs created a similar impression with a mock attack on the Kuwaiti coast near Mina Saud.

The ground assault to liberate Kuwait began at 0400 on 24 February. I MEF thrust directly toward its ultimate objective, the al-Mutla Pass and the roads leading from Kuwait City. Over the next four days, the Marines breached both Iraqi defensive belts in Kuwait, fought their way through pockets of stiff enemy resistance, and fended off several armored counterattacks on their drive north. The Army's XVIII and VII Corps executed their massive envelopment maneuver, rumbling north into Iraq then east to attack the Republican Guard units arrayed north of Kuwait. By 0800 on 28 February, Army units had won several fierce tank battles and had reached a position 30 miles west of Basra. Meanwhile, Arab forces of the Joint Forces Commands–North and East had secured most of their objectives in Kuwait and had liberated the Kuwaiti capital.

Central Command dedicated numerous aircraft sorties to support the ground offensive. Although no U.S. Navy or non-U.S. coalition fixed-wing aircraft participated in close air support, they did fly interdiction missions during the ground campaign. At first, interdiction missions aimed at disrupting counterattacks on allied ground forces. Later, the focus shifted to destruction of a fleeing enemy. By the end of the first 48 hours, the front lines had moved so far north that Navy pilots shifted their attacks to Iraqi forces north of Kuwait City. Aircraft from Battle Force Zulu also struck targets on Failaka Island to support amphibious deception operations.

On 25 February, the amphibious task force conducted a fake amphibious landing just north of the Kuwaiti port of Ash Shuaybah, involving gunfire from the battleship *Missouri*, a feint by helicopters of the 13th Marine Expeditionary Unit (MEU),

and charges detonated by SEALs along the beach. At 0452, an Iraqi Silkworm battery near al-Fintas fired two missiles at the bombardment group. One of the Silkworms splashed down near *Missouri*, possibly falling short because of countermeasures taken by the ships. The British destroyer *Gloucester* shot down the second Silkworm with two Sea Dart missiles. Naval air forces destroyed the Silkworm launch site. The next morning, helicopters from amphibious ships *Nassau* (LHA 4), *Guam* (LPH 9), and *Iwo Jima* (LPH 2) made feints toward Bubiyan and Failaka islands. The amphibious deception operations worked. Central Command later estimated that the operations pinned down 70,000–80,000 Iraqi troops—more than six divisions.

By daybreak on 27 February, I MEF had secured all of its objectives. Leathernecks consolidated their positions and began to mop up the last pockets of enemy resistance. Organized Iraqi action within Kuwait City ceased. Arab forces passed through Marine lines to liberate Kuwait City. President Bush ordered the cessation of offensive operations at 0800 on 28 February 1991 (Arabian Gulf time)—100 hours after the final assault had begun.

Coalition forces ceased offensive military operations at the appointed hour but stood by to resume fighting if necessary. Central Command and the Defense Intelligence Agency assessed 33 Iraqi divisions as combat ineffective. Most Iraqi army units had surrendered, had been destroyed, or had fled. U.S. losses were miraculously few. In all, between 3 August 1990 and 15 December 1991, the United States lost 313 dead as a result of Operations Desert Shield and Desert Storm. Of these, the Navy lost 56 Sailors. In return for their sacrifice, the coalition had won one of the most decisive victories in military history.

Desert Shield and Desert Storm were pivotal operations in the history of Naval Forces Central Command. Not only did naval forces play a decisive role in the coalition's victory, but the Gulf War accelerated the Navy's transition from a Cold War, blue-water focus to a post-Cold War littoral focus, convinced the Navy to become a better player in the joint arena, and reaffirmed the Navy's commitment to the Arabian Gulf region. +++

ENFORCING THE PEACE

SADDAM HUSSEIN WORKED EXTENSIVELY to evade the economic sanctions and military restrictions imposed on his regime by the U.N. coalition after Desert Storm. Violence erupted periodically as the United States implemented its policy to contain and disarm his regime. Naval Forces Central Command played a key role in enforcing the peace.

In March 1991, Kurds in northern Iraq and Shiites in the south rebelled against the Baathist government. The revolt revealed the hatred for Saddam that years of repression, torture, and murder had built up among Iraq's Shiites and Kurds.

The uprising confronted the regime with the most serious internal challenge it had ever faced. For a time the rebels seemed to be winning. Kurdish guerrillas gained control of three northern provinces and the important oil center of Kirkuk, while rebellion spread through all of the major Shiite cities and towns of the south, including Basra and the holy cities Najaf and Karbala. Angry Iraqi soldiers returning from the debacle in Kuwait took part in the rebellion.

Saddam Hussein retaliated by inflicting massive atrocities on his people. Enough Iraqi heavy equipment had survived Desert Storm to equip seven to nine divisions, and some twenty Iraqi divisions had not seen combat during the war. Although Iraq's army had been virtually impotent against Western forces, these remnants crushed the lightly armed Kurds

Tents cover a mountainside in the Kurdish refugee camp of Yekmel during Operation Provide Comfort, 11 May 1991.

PH2 (AC) Mark Kettenhofen

and Shiites. While retaking cities and consolidating control in rebellious areas, loyalist forces fired indiscriminately into residential areas; demolished many prominent Shiite shrines and institutions; executed people on the streets, in their homes, and in hospitals; gunned them down with helicopters; and hanged them from tank guns. Thousands of men, women, and children perished. Hamstrung by rules of engagement that disallowed unprovoked movement into unoccupied portions of Iraq, American forces could not intervene to stop the slaughter.

Saddam's brutal retribution precipitated one of the largest flights of refugees in modern times, an exodus of over 10 percent of Iraq's population. An estimated 1.4 million Iraqis fled to Iran, 450,000 to Turkey, 35,000 to Saudi Arabia and Kuwait, and smaller numbers to Syria and Jordan. In the inhospitable mountain areas of Iraq, Iran, and Turkey, refugees died at a rate of 2,000 per day from dehydration, malnutrition, disease, and exposure.

On 5 April 1991, the United Nations passed Resolution 688, which demanded that Saddam

Aviation ordnancemen take cover after hooking containers to an SH-60F helicopter on the flight deck of the carrier Harry S. Truman *(CVN 75), on station in the Arabian Gulf, 20 April 2001.*

stop committing atrocities and permit unhampered humanitarian assistance to refugees. That same day, military forces from 11 nations, led by the U.S. European Command, launched Operation Provide Comfort to aid the refugees in northern Iraq and southern Turkey. Elements of the combined task force, about 20,000 people, including 11,000 American service men and women, mostly Army personnel, entered northern Iraq in mid-April. The coalition warned Baghdad not to resist the movement, not to fly aircraft in a "no-fly zone" established north of the 36th parallel, and not to send troops into a "security zone" along the border with Turkey. Having just taken a beating and not inclined to risk another, Saddam complied. Refugees

fleeing to southern Iran and the occupied portion of southern Iraq also received food, tents, cots, blankets, water, clothing, and medical attention from coalition forces. In the north, the presence of coalition troops made the Kurds feel safe enough to return to their homes or to special "way station" camps set up near Zakho. By mid-June, almost all of the refugees had left the squalid, mountaintop camps along the Turkey-Iraq border.

Following withdrawal of coalition ground forces from northern Iraq in mid-July, coalition air units, including carrier aircraft flying from the Mediterranean, continued to patrol the northern no-fly zone. After Provide Comfort officially ended in December 1996, coalition aircraft out of Incirlik Air Base, Turkey, enforced the northern no-fly zone under Operation Northern Watch.

Despite Saddam's brutality in crushing the rebellion, Shiites in the vast marshlands lying between the lower reaches of the Tigris and Euphrates rivers in southern Iraq remained restive. The Madan People, or Marsh Arabs, as the region's inhabitants were known, had a distinctive culture based on farming, fishing, and hunting dating back thousands of years. The marshes, because of their terrain and proximity to Iran, had long served as a sanctuary for criminals and others hiding from the central authorities, such as deserters from the Iraqi army during the war with Iran. By the spring of 1992, the marshes contained the largest concentration of active resistance fighters in southern Iraq, with rebel commanders claiming 10,000 fighters. The number was doubtless exaggerated, since the rebels mounted little more than sporadic hit-and-run attacks.

Nevertheless, Saddam determined to eliminate all resistance in the region. In early 1992, Baghdad ordered major counterinsurgency operations against the Marsh Arabs. That spring, brigade-size ground and air forces launched search and destroy operations in southern Iraq. To facilitate these operations, gain greater political control over the area, and punish the insurgents, the Baathist government launched a civil engineering project to drain the marshes and thereby to destroy the Madan People's way of life.

Since Saddam's campaign against the Marsh Arabs violated Resolution 688, on 26 August 1992, the United States, United Kingdom, and France established a no-fly zone in southern Iraq, barring flights of Iraqi aircraft south of the 32nd parallel. The next day, U.S. naval and air forces launched Operation Southern Watch. This operation aimed at preventing Iraqi aircraft from threatening Iraqi Shiites and neighboring countries as well as at blocking cargo airplanes from delivering to Iraq technologies applicable to weapons of mass destruction (WMD). On 27 August, naval aircraft from *Independence* and *Tarawa* (LHA 1), operating in the Arabian Gulf, began flying combat air patrols and reconnaissance missions over southern Iraq, ready to shoot down any Iraqi aircraft that trespassed into the southern no-fly zone. At that time, 23 U.S. naval vessels and more than 13,000 men and women were on hand in NAVCENT's area of responsibility to support Southern Watch. U.S. Air Force, British, and French planes also participated in the effort.

Marine General Joseph P. Hoar, who had succeeded General Schwarzkopf as CINCCENT in September 1991, established a task force organization, designated Joint Task Force Southwest Asia (JTF-SWA), to manage Southern Watch and to plan for other contingencies. Because Central Command Air Forces then operated the greatest number of American aircraft in the theater, General Hoar directed Lieutenant General Michael A. Nelson, his Air Force component commander, to lead the task force.

During Southern Watch, the Navy resolved the joint organizational and operational problems that had arisen during Desert Storm. Instead of sending relatively junior officers to the JTF-SWA staff, the Navy assigned as General Nelson's deputy Rear Admiral David N. Rogers, who was then COMUSNAVCENT-Rear, a billet created during a NAVCENT reorganization in April 1991. Although Air Force officers predominated in the 200-person JTF-SWA staff, naval officers participated fully in

An F-14D Tomcat launches from George Washington *(CVN 73) for a mission in support of Operation Southern Watch, 3 September 2000.*

Airman Kumba Calvin secures a sling during crash and salvage training on the flight deck of Harry S. Truman *on station in the Arabian Gulf, 20 April 2001.*

the planning and targeting functions, with Navy captains serving as deputies of the key Intelligence (J-2) and Operations (J-3) staff positions.

The Navy, Army, and Marine Corps agreed that the Joint Forces Air Component Commander should be in control of Southern Watch. When naval aircraft took off from a carrier to patrol the no-fly zone, they "chopped" (change in operational control) to the JFACC with no difficulty. The task force staff employed an air tasking order for every flying operation, including all air defense, air control, and rescue missions in the operational area. The fleet did not maintain separate control as it had for the latter missions during the Gulf War. Moreover, the Navy had dramatically improved the communications and data link systems on board the carriers since Desert Storm, so working with the shore-based task force headquarters in refining the ATO presented no major

problems. Navy strike planners on board *La Salle* and the carrier task force assigned to Central Command received the ATO electronically. In contrast to the Desert Storm experience, the Navy's involvement in joint air operations and the ATO process did not generate anxiety among naval staff officers.

The coalition forbade Iraq from taking hostile action against coalition aircraft patrolling the no-fly zone, though Saddam's government denied it was bound by the rule and routinely attempted to shoot down coalition fighters it said were intruding in its sovereign airspace. In early September 1992, Navy EA-6B Prowler aircraft and other sources detected a rise in Iraqi air defense activity within the no-fly zone and an increased tempo of Iraqi air operations above the 32nd parallel. The coalition responded to this threat with a show of force to preempt any Iraqi moves to disrupt Southern Watch. U.S., British, and French planes, flying in a combined formation for the first time on 9 September, flooded the air over southern Iraq. The threatening Iraqi air defense activity soon subsided.

In early November, the nuclear attack submarine *Topeka* (SSN 754), armed with Tomahawks, added a new dimension to the Navy's presence in the littoral areas of the world when she joined the carrier battle group participating in Southern Watch. This deployment marked the first instance of a nuclear-powered U.S. submarine operating in the shallow waters of the Arabian Gulf.

In late December, the Iraqis began positioning and activating antiaircraft missile batteries south of the 32nd parallel. They also warned coalition pilots flying over Iraq that they would shoot down any intruding planes. Then, the batteries fired on allied aircraft over both no-fly zones. On 6 January 1993, shortly before turning over power to President-elect William J. Clinton, President Bush delivered an ultimatum to Saddam to remove the missiles from the southern no-fly zone within 48 hours or suffer the consequences. The Iraqis replied by expropriating four Silkworm missiles and other military equipment from a portion of their former naval base at Umm Qasr that they had ceded to Kuwait as part of the Gulf War settlement.

A KC-135R Stratotanker refuels an F/A-18 Hornet as an F-14A Tomcat waits its turn during their Southern Watch no-fly-zone patrol mission, 1 February 1993.

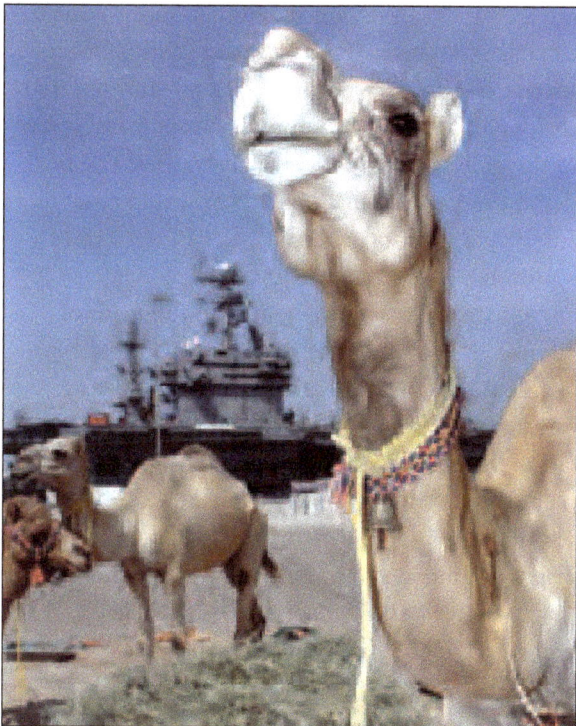

Camels graze on grass near the docks at the port of Jebel Ali, United Arab Emirates. The carrier Carl Vinson *(CVN 70) looms in the background.*

The allies responded quickly. On 13 January 1993, 35 U.S. Navy warplanes from the carrier *Kitty Hawk* (CV 63), which had arrived in the Arabian Gulf on New Year's Day, along with 75 U.S. Air Force, British, and French aircraft, attacked four air defense command and control centers and two concentrations of SA-3 surface-to-air missiles in the southern no-fly zone. Iraqi antiaircraft fire missed the planes, while the coalition aircraft destroyed only one mobile battery.

On 17 January, Iraqi antiaircraft artillery, missile batteries, and fighters once again threatened allied planes, this time in northern Iraq. The hostile aircraft repeatedly darted back and forth across the 36th parallel, attempting to draw allied planes toward surface-to-air missile batteries just below the boundary. No allied Airmen took the bait.

Again, the coalition responded quickly. Later that day, cruiser *Cowpens* (CG 63) and destroyers *Hewitt* (DD 966) and *Stump* (DD 978), operating in the Arabian Gulf, and destroyer *Caron* (DD 970), steaming in the Red Sea, launched 42 Tomahawk

Aviation Electronics Technician Airman Shannon Ireland maintains an F/A-18 Hornet on the flight deck of Carl Vinson, *operating in the Arabian Gulf, 5 March 1999.*

cruise missiles against a multibillion-dollar factory complex in Zaafaraniyah, about eight miles southeast of Baghdad. This facility contained computer-operated precision machine tools that had been used to enrich uranium for Iraq's nuclear weapons program. At least 30 Tomahawks got through, hitting every one of the targeted structures. U.S. Air Force F-15Es also severely damaged the Tallil Station Air Operations Center.

Saddam had had enough. The next day, the eve of President Clinton's inauguration, Baghdad declared a cease-fire and informed the United Nations that it would no longer attempt to restrict flights of U.N. weapons inspectors inside Iraq.

Only temporarily chastened, that spring Saddam sent a covert team into Kuwait to kill former President Bush, who was then visiting the emirate. As a result of the failed assassination attempt, the National Command Authority called on NAVCENT to increase the pressure on the Iraqi dictator. On 26 June 1993, the cruiser *Chancellorsville* (CG 62) in the Arabian Gulf and the destroyer *Peterson* (DD 969) in the Red Sea successfully launched 23 Tomahawks against an intelligence headquarters in the Iraqi capital. The TLAMs scored at least 13 hits and severely damaged the targeted buildings. Without risking the lives of any pilots, the Navy in the gulf once again enforced Washington's will to restrain Saddam.

In the fall of 1994, Saddam began maneuvering Republican Guard armored and other forces toward Iraq's border with Kuwait. On 6 October, American intelligence analysts concluded that Iraq would be capable of attacking Kuwait with five divisions in seven days. President Clinton immediately ordered the deployment of U.S. ground, air, and naval forces to the gulf in Operation Vigilant Warrior. The next day, he announced that U.S. forces would resist any Iraqi aggression. Military Sealift Command's maritime prepositioning ships at Diego Garcia and Guam set sail for the gulf with full loads of ammunition, equipment, and supplies. The *George Washington* (CVN 73) carrier battle group, then operating off Bosnia, soon joined the naval forces already in position in the theater. These forces included ten surface ships and an attack submarine, with hundreds of Tomahawks among them, and the *Tripoli* amphibious ready group (ARG), with the 15th MEU (Special Operations Capable [SOC]) embarked. During this operation, 6,400 naval and 301 Air Force personnel reinforced the 6,600 Sailors and Marines and 4,000 Air Force men and women already in the Central Command area of responsibility.

PHAN John Sullivan

Lieutenant Chris Adams straps on his F-14 Tomcat prior to engine start on board Independence (CV 62) *during Operation Southern Watch, 17 April 1998.*

PH3 James W. Olive

Front to back: Cruisers Lake Erie (CG 70) *and* Chosin (CG 65), *ammunition ship* Mount Hood (AE 29), *and oiler* Cimarron (AO 177) *steam toward the NAVCENT area of responsibility, 14 April 1997.*

During the first days of the crisis, Marine forces constituted more than 50 percent of the American ground troops in the gulf. Moreover, during the first two weeks of the crisis, Navy and Marine Corps units accounted for 60 percent of the combat-ready U.S. aircraft in the region. These forces were not overwhelming, but their quick reaction to the Iraqi threat proved sufficient to convince Saddam of American resolve. Accordingly, long before major U.S. land-based ground and air forces reached the theater, delayed by overflight and basing problems, intelligence assets sighted Iraqi trains carrying hundreds of armored vehicles headed away from the Kuwait border.

Saddam Hussein's postwar provocations continued to threaten peace in the Arabian Gulf region, but the quick and effective U.S. military response in each episode, routinely involving Naval Forces Central Command, prevented a return to the unfavorable balance of power that existed in August 1990. The coalition's continuing vigilance and readiness to resist Iraqi aggression in the wake of Desert Storm paid huge dividends for stability in the Arabian Gulf. +++

ESTABLISHMENT OF FIFTH FLEET
AND EVOLUTION OF NSA BAHRAIN

WHILE ENFORCING THE PEACE, the Navy incorporated lessons learned from the Gulf War into NAVCENT's command structure. The principal lesson involved a cultural shift away from the Navy's preference to operate in support of Central Command toward joint operations as part of Central Command. This shift culminated on 1 July 1995 in the establishment of the Fifth Fleet, the first stand-up of a fighting fleet in a half-century.

In the wake of Desert Storm, Vice Admiral Arthur encouraged the Navy to institutionalize some of the lessons learned during the war. He was especially interested in reorganizing the NAVCENT command structure to facilitate jointness, particularly in improving COMUSNAVCENT's relationships to the theater headquarters and the other component commanders. The war, he declared, "has shown the absolute need for a Navy component commander that has the staff, connectivity, and seniority to command a large naval presence."

On 9 March 1991, Admiral Arthur proposed a reorganization scheme to General Schwarzkopf to make his successor as COMUSNAVCENT a two-star naval officer "dual-hatted" as Commander Middle East Force. Because of its historical legacy and legitimacy in the eyes of America's gulf allies, he reasoned, the Middle East Force should retain its identity. In the event of another large crisis, COMUSNAVCENT would relocate his headquarters with Commander in Chief, Central Command.

Rear Admiral Raynor A. K. Taylor assumed command of NAVCENT on 24 April 1991. Taylor was dual-hatted as Arthur had suggested and

headquartered on board *La Salle*, home-ported in Bahrain, thus becoming Central Command's only forward-deployed component commander. At the same time, Rear Admiral Robert Sutton became COMUSNAVCENT-Rear. That July, Rear Admiral David Rogers relieved Sutton and COMUSNAVCENT-Rear and his staff relocated to Tampa, Florida.

Admiral Frank B. Kelso II, Chief of Naval Operations, reasoned that a two-star admiral would lack the seniority necessary to command a large naval force in wartime, so the Pacific Fleet or the Atlantic Fleet would still have to provide a three-star flag officer to Central Command. Admiral Kelso decided to assign permanently a three-star flag officer to lead NAVCENT. On 19 October 1992, Vice Admiral Douglas Katz succeeded Rear Admiral Taylor. The assignment of a three-star flag officer symbolized the Navy's acknowledgment of the need for a fully developed naval component within Central Command. That same year, the Administrative Support Unit Bahrain was renamed Administrative Support Unit Southwest Asia (ASU-SWA).

Idaho (BB 42) fires its 14-inch guns at targets on Okinawa, 1 April 1945. Today's Fifth Fleet is the namesake of the World War II fleet in which this battleship served.

U.S. Naval Historical Center

Bahrain.

Naval Support Activity Bahrain front gate.

After serving as COMUSNAVCENT flagship for 21 years, *La Salle* departed Bahrain for the last time on 10 April 1993. She was overhauled in Philadelphia and then reassigned to the Sixth Fleet as flagship.

When *La Salle* departed, the NAVCENT staff moved into a trailer village prepared by the ASU-SWA Public Works Department. The admiral and his staff no longer needed a flagship, for COMUSNAVCENT intended to remain ashore in Bahrain permanently. In the event of war, they planned to relocate with CINCCENT in Riyadh. Any of the carriers assigned to NAVCENT could readily handle the communications needed to direct forces afloat.

In September 1994, Vice Admiral John Scott Redd succeeded Katz as COMUSNAVCENT. The naval component commander's duties had long included keeping watch on the military and political situation within the command's area of responsibility. With Iraq and Iran still threatening peace and stability in the region, and carrier battle groups and amphibious ready groups operating in the AOR routinely, Admiral Redd and other naval leaders advocated establishing a fleet command.

Back in the states, OPNAV, the Office of the Secretary of Defense, the Joint Staff, and State Department debated the merits of establishing another fleet. Proponents argued that to do so would broadcast a strong signal of commitment to the region, function as an echelon between COMUSNAVCENT and the operating forces, and involve minimal staff augmentation. Opponents questioned the need for a new fleet at a time when the Navy was retiring dozens of warships. The proponents made the better case. On 4 May 1995, Secretary of Defense William J. Perry approved the stand-up of a new fighting fleet, designated Fifth Fleet.

The Navy drew upon its World War II heritage for the designation. On 15 March 1943, Admiral Ernest J. King, Commander in Chief, United States Fleet, established numbered fleets as a basis for task force designations and for specific geographic areas. He designated Fifth Fleet to operate in the Central Pacific Ocean and placed Vice Admiral Raymond A. Spruance in command. Fifth Fleet fought some of the war's most significant battles, including Philippine Sea, Iwo Jima, and Okinawa. In March 1945, Commander Seventh Fleet assumed responsibilities for the control of the areas and the forces assigned to Fifth Fleet, and the staff moved ashore to the West Coast. It remained there until January 1947, when the Navy disestablished Fifth Fleet as part of the general postwar drawdown of naval forces worldwide.

On 1 July 1995, the Navy formally stood up the Fifth Fleet during a small ceremony at Admiral Redd's office. The commander of Destroyer Squadron 50 became dual-hatted as Commander Middle East Force. The reestablishment of Fifth Fleet brought the naval organization in Central Command in line with the Pacific Command, which had the Third and Seventh fleets; the Atlantic Command, which had the Second Fleet; and the European Command, which had the Sixth Fleet. As Secretary of State Warren Christopher put it, the

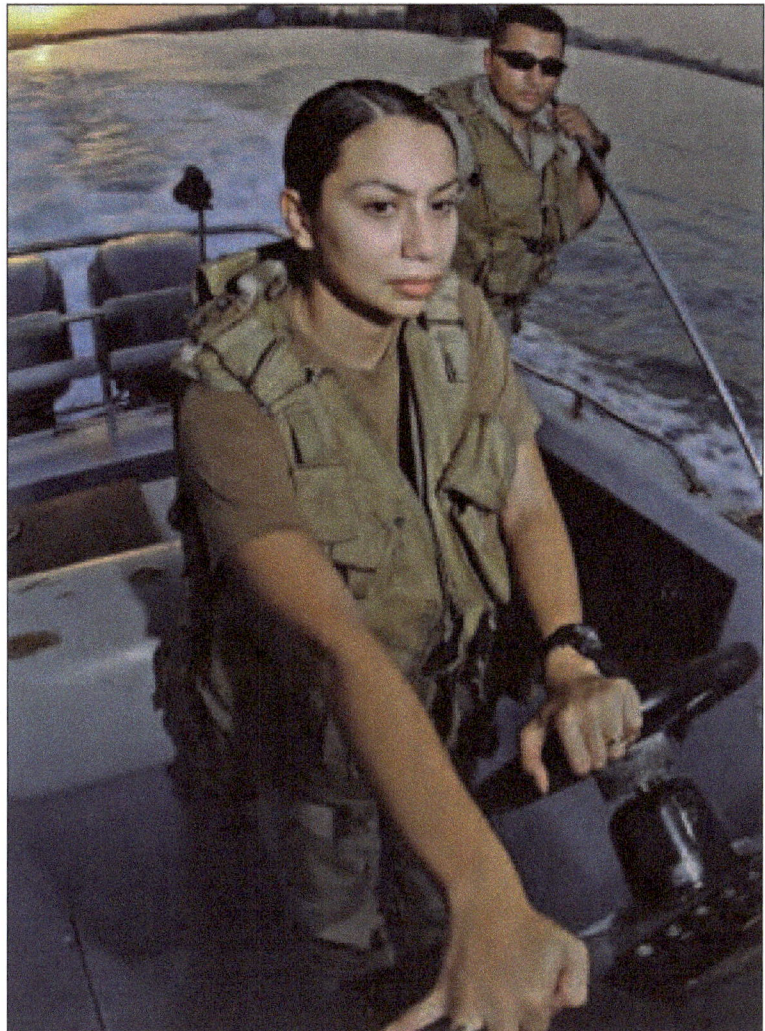

Quartermaster 2nd Class Carolina Castanon, a Sailor in Naval Support Activity Bahrain's Harbor Patrol Unit, makes her rounds, 28 September 2003.

stand-up of Fifth Fleet demonstrated that the Navy's commitment to the region was "ironclad."

In the new organization scheme, naval forces deployed from the Pacific and Atlantic fleets to the region, where they came under operational control of the Fifth Fleet. Commander Fifth Fleet was subordinate to and an additional duty of COMUSNAVCENT. The dual-hatted naval component commander reported to CINCCENT for contingency planning and operational matters and to the Chief of Naval Operations for administrative concerns.

As they developed Fifth Fleet's task organization, Admiral Redd and his staff established Task Force 50, which included all combatants in

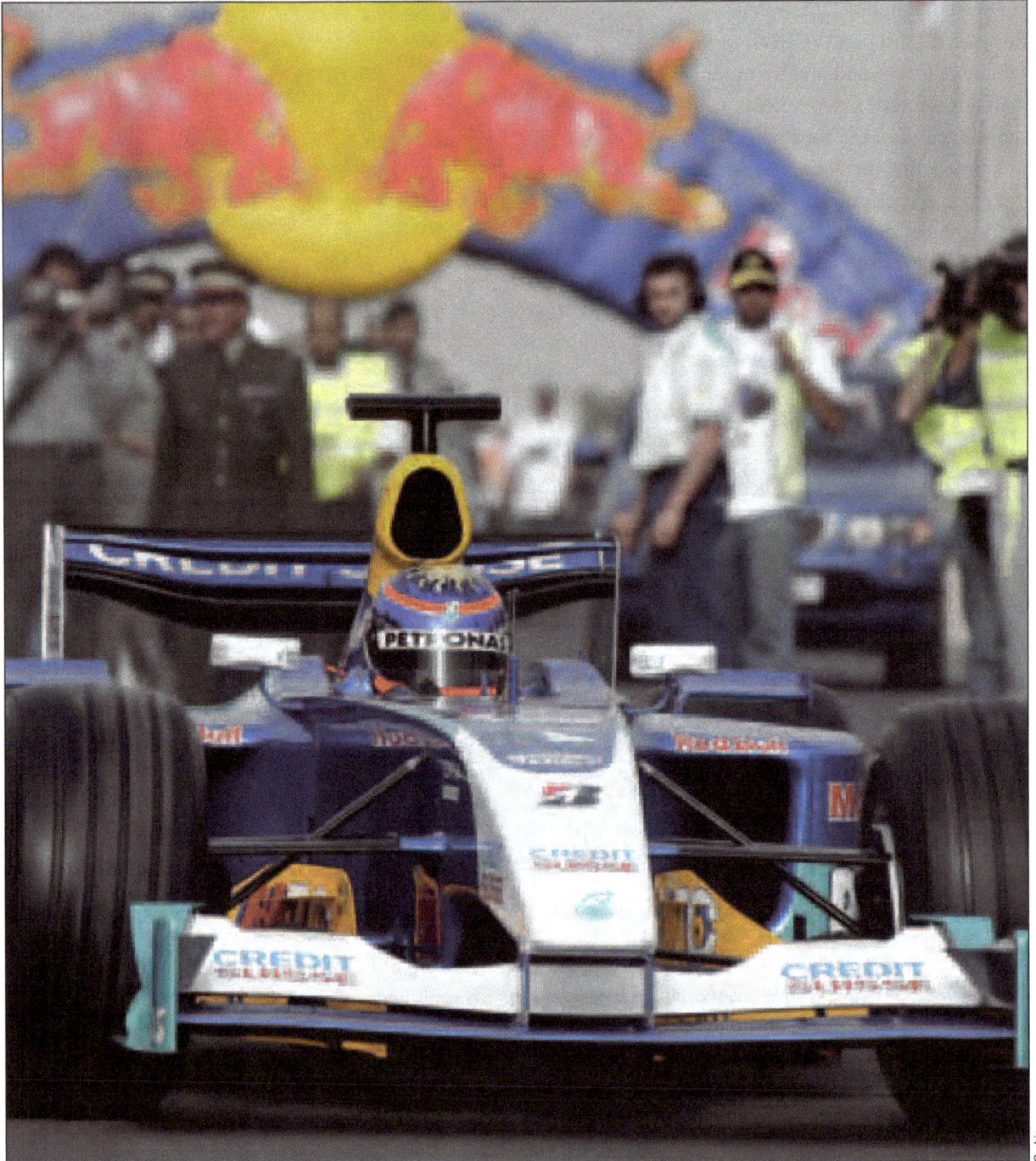

Corbis

Nico Janni drives his Petronas-Saubeer Formula One car at high-speed on Bahrain's King Faisal Highway. In 2004 the island hosted its first F1 race at the most advanced racing facility of its kind in the world.

the gulf during day-to-day operations. In the event of a major theater war or other large operational contingency, Fifth Fleet would transition to traditional task organizations. From its inception, Fifth Fleet considered joint and combined operations to be of paramount importance.

On 1 January 1996, the Department of Defense added to the CENTCOM area of responsibility the entire Arabian Sea and a portion of the Indian Ocean running south from Pakistan to near Diego Garcia and west from Diego Garcia to the coast of southern Kenya. On 5 August 1999, Administrative

Actor and comedian Robin Williams performs during an all-hands gathering at Naval Support Activity Bahrain, 19 December 2003.

Support Unit Southwest Asia was redesignated Naval Support Activity (NSA) Bahrain, a name denoting facilities that provide direct support to the fleet and reflecting the Navy's permanent presence in the Arabian Gulf.

Although the organization had evolved, the mission remained the same: ensuring stability in the region, countering the proliferation of weapons of mass destruction, and ensuring access to strategic natural resources.

The Navy's facilities in Bahrain, however, underwent substantial change. When Fifth Fleet stood up, a combination of old British-era stucco buildings and temporary prefabricated metal buildings dotted the 23-acre naval base. On 25 June 1996, terrorists bombed the Khobar Towers, an apartment complex housing Central Command personnel in Dhahran, Saudi Arabia, killing 19

Americans and wounding hundreds more. The blast was so powerful that many people in Bahrain felt the concussion. NAVCENT immediately launched a $6 million program to beef up force protection in Bahrain. Two Marine Corps platoon-size Fleet Antiterrorism Security Teams (FASTs) augmented existing Navy and Bahraini security forces by 4 July. The next month COMUSNAVCENT worked with the U.S. Ambassador to Bahrain to obtain 45 acres of land adjacent to the compound.

In the years that followed, the Army Corps of Engineers, with assistance from Naval Facilities Engineering Command and the base's Public Works Center, launched a construction program expected to total approximately $200 million by the year 2010. The program sought to facilitate operations and force protection while improving quality of life at NSA Bahrain. The construction

Vice Admiral David C. Nichols Jr. addresses Sailors during the change of command ceremony outside Fifth Fleet headquarters in which Vice Admiral Patrick M. Walsh relieved him as Commander U.S. Naval Forces Central Command/Fifth Fleet, 3 November 2005.

followed a master plan drafted after the Khobar Towers tragedy to move the activities with the largest staffs into a triangular area set well inside the base. The original 23 acres were cleared of vehicular traffic and became a pedestrian-only zone. A wall and guard towers designed to blend with local architecture were constructed around the base perimeter. Reinforced concrete "townhouses" were built to house several of the 42 tenant commands. Construction finished by 2005 included barracks; a medical and dental clinic; recreation, shopping, and banking facilities; and a childcare center. The jewel of the construction program was the 128,144-square-foot, $25 million headquarters complex that opened for business on 4 January 2004.

The building program made a significant impact on the local economy. Before the Gulf War, no more than 100 Sailors had been stationed in Bahrain.

By the fall of 2001, some 1,200 military men and women worked at the base. Not only did the building program benefit Bahraini contractors engaged in construction projects on base, but a huge new market for hotels, apartments, restaurants, and entertainment sprang up almost overnight. Juffair became Bahrain's boomtown. For security reasons, the Navy placed strict limits on the number of Americans permitted to stay in each hotel or apartment. Building owners had to get non-Navy clients to fill up the rest of their space. As fortune had it, the Navy's expansion coincided with Manama's rise as the hub of commerce and banking in the region.

Bahrain wasn't the only Arabian Gulf nation whose economy benefited from the Navy's presence. Before Desert Storm, no Arab nations other than Bahrain and Oman had granted U.S. forces the right to use shore facilities on a regular basis. By 2003,

Vice Admiral Patrick Walsh tours Naval Support Activity Bahrain with Bahrain's Crown Prince, His Highness Sheikh Salman bin Hamad bin Isa al-Khalifa, 28 November 2006. During the Crown Prince's visit, Admiral Walsh discussed the Navy's role in the Middle East as well as relations between Bahrain and the U.S. military.

Situated on the King Faisal Highway close to Juffair, the al-Fateh Mosque, also called the Grand Mosque, is Bahrain's largest religious building. Visitors are allowed to enter the mosque throughout the day, except during prayer times.

however, the U.S. Navy used the shore facilities of all the GCC states. Throughout the 1990s, the United Arab Emirates welcomed U.S. naval warships on port and liberty calls and opened its huge Jebel Ali port facility to aircraft carriers for visits and repairs. For much of the 1990s the UAE also hosted U.S. air refueling assets, which supported Air Force and Navy sorties in Operation Southern Watch. U.S. Navy P-3s began flying maritime interception operations out of Masirah, Oman, in 1990.

The establishment of a new fleet, construction of extensive new base facilities in Bahrain, and use of facilities throughout the region emphasized the permanence of the Navy's presence in the Arabian Gulf. Just as the presence of the Sixth Fleet in the Mediterranean during the Cold War reflected a resolve to maintain order and stability in Europe, so too did the rechristening of the U.S. Fifth Fleet signal a resolve to maintain order and stability in the Arabian Gulf region. +++

HUMANITARIAN OPERATIONS

SINCE ITS BIRTH IN 1775, the United States Navy has existed primarily to fight in war or to prepare for war. Throughout its history, the Navy also employed ships and aircraft for humanitarian purposes. After the establishment of the Middle East Force in 1949, the Navy not only compiled a war-winning record in the Arabian Gulf region but also established a reputation for helping people in need, from mariners in distress to civilians ashore suffering from natural or man-made disasters.

Ships assigned to the Middle East Force and to Naval Forces Central Command have answered countless distress calls. In June 1950, for example, an Air France DC-4 airliner crashed on approach to the Bahrain airfield. Sailors from *Greenwich Bay* were the first to arrive on the scene and rescued nine passengers. In 1955, Sailors from *Valcour* boarded the blazing and abandoned Italian tanker *Argea Primato* and extinguished the fire, thus averting a major environmental disaster. When devastating floods swept through Ceylon in 1957, Sailors on board *Duxbury Bay* rushed food, supplies, and medical personnel to the disaster area; coordinated the efforts of other ships assigned to help; and helped prevent the outbreak of epidemics. In 1962, crewmen from *Duxbury Bay* and the destroyer *Soley* (DD 707) assisted a mariner from the Danish tanker *Prima Maersk* who had suffered third degree burns in an engine room fire. In 1974, the destroyer escort *Capodanno* (DE 1093) assisted three Kenyan patrol boats running low on fuel in

A Kurdish man watches American forces arrive at a refugee camp near Zakho, Iraq, during Operation Provide Comfort, 1 May 1991.

PH2(AC) Mark Kettenhofen

high seas. *Capodanno* transferred fuel to the boats, took one under tow for a brief time when it suffered an engineering casualty, and escorted all three safely to Mombasa, Kenya's principal port. In 1998, Sailors from the frigate *Gary* (FFG 51), destroyer *Harry W. Hill* (DD 986), and oiler *Tippecanoe* (T-AO 199) treated a badly burned mariner from the merchantman *British Harrier* and then transferred him to a hospital ashore. In August 2000, the carrier *George Washington*, destroyer *Oldendorf* (DD 972), USNS *Catawba* (T-ATF 168), and Helicopter Combat Support Special Squadron Two, Detachment Two conducted a search and recovery mission following the crash of Gulf Air Airbus 320. On 2 January 2004, a helicopter from the cruiser *Gettysburg* (CG 64) medevaced to the carrier *Enterprise* (CVN 65) an Iraqi seaman seriously injured when a cable parted while his freighter was towing another ship. The list of instances of U.S. ships aiding mariners in distress is already long and will only grow in the years to come.

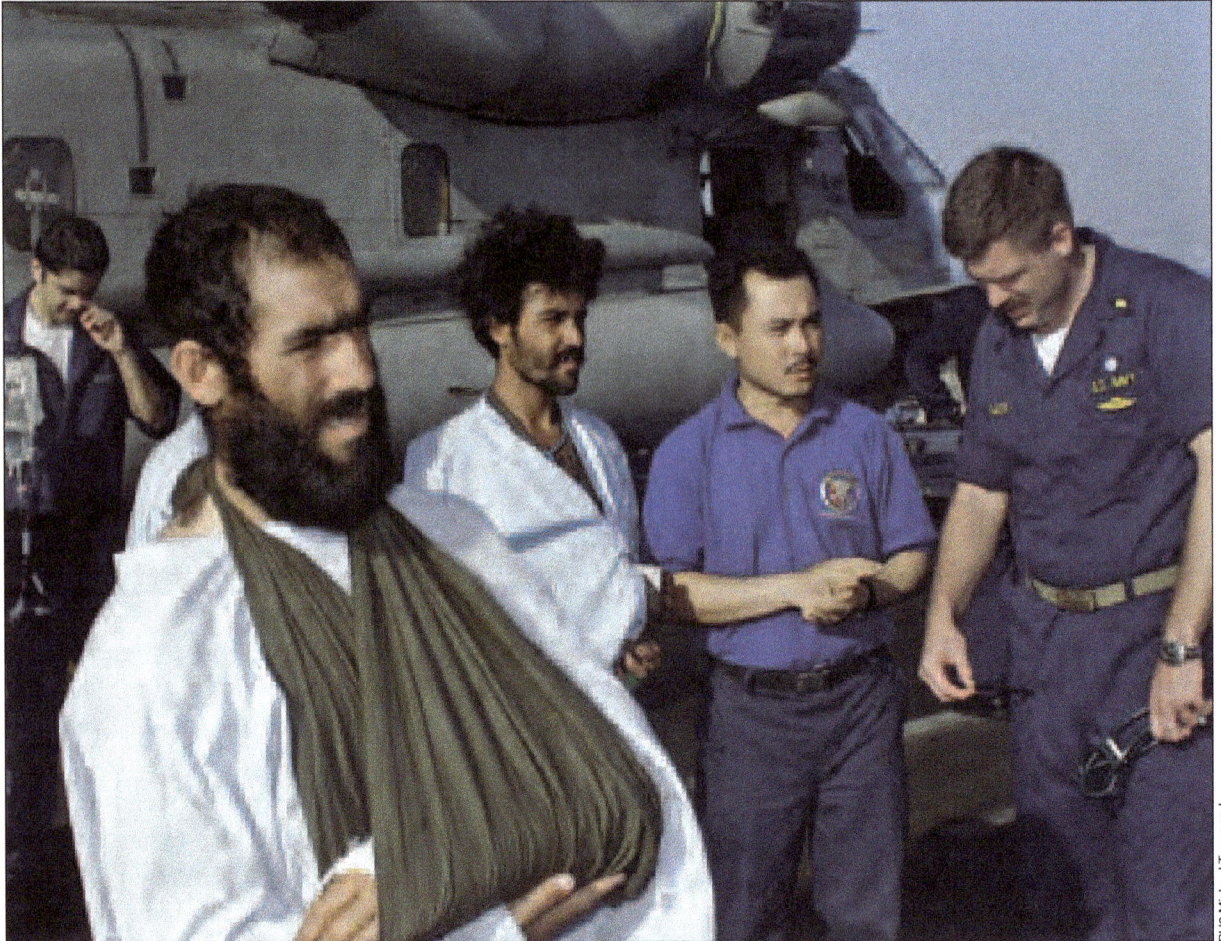

Wounded anti-Taliban fighters get some fresh air and sunshine on the flight deck of the amphibious ship Peleliu *(LHA 5), 9 December 2001. Many Afghanis who received medical treatment on board the ship had never before seen the ocean.*

Ships en route to or outbound from the NAVCENT area of responsibility have frequently participated in relief efforts sparked by natural disasters. In May 1991, while on the way home after serving in the Gulf War, Amphibious Group Three, with the 5th MEB embarked, paused off Bangladesh to participate in Operation Sea Angel, after a cyclone devastated that nation during the last two days of April. While en route to the Arabian Gulf region in January 2005, the amphibious assault ship *Bonhomme Richard* (LHD 6), flagship of Expeditionary Strike Group (ESG) 5, and the embarked 15th MEU, conducted nine days of humanitarian assistance operations in support of Operation Unified Assistance, delivering more than a million pounds of humanitarian aid to tsunami survivors on the Indonesian island of Sumatra.

In the decade after Desert Storm, some of the most significant challenges facing NAVCENT involved the east African nation of Somalia. After years of political unrest, in January 1991, rebels overthrew the repressive regime of dictator Mohammed Siad Barre. Violence continued unabated as civil war broke out among 14 clans and sub-clans vying for power.

On 5 January, the *Guam* and *Trenton* (LPD 14) amphibious ready groups, with elements of the 4th MEB embarked, arrived off the Somali capital, Mogadishu. COMUSNAVCENT had deployed the ships from the Arabian Gulf where they had been supporting Operation Desert Shield. That night, in Operation Eastern Exit, Marine Corps helicopters evacuated 281 people, representing 30 countries, from the U.S. Embassy in Mogadishu.

Horn of Africa.

Lieutenant Amy Plant, a Navy dentist, examines an Afghan boy during a civil affairs project in the village of Najoy, Afghanistan, 22 April 2004.

Meanwhile, an ongoing east African drought ravaged the Somali people. The combination of drought and civil war proved disastrous. Non-governmental organizations (NGOs) such as the International Red Cross and the Red Crescent Society struggled in vain to stabilize the situation and provide food and other humanitarian assistance. Widespread looting, fighting between gangs, and other lawlessness, however, prevented 80 percent of relief supplies from reaching the hungry and sick. An estimated 25 percent of Somalia's six million people died of starvation or disease. Famine and fighting displaced approximately two million people from their homes. Refugees fled to neighboring countries or to urban areas. All institutions of governance and at least 60 percent of the country's basic infrastructure disintegrated.

In 1992, the United Nations took action to try to help the stricken nation. The Security Council imposed an arms embargo on Somalia, brokered cease-fire agreements between the rival parties, and established United Nations Operation Somalia (UNOSOM) to monitor the cease-fire and to convoy supplies.

Nevertheless, the situation in Somalia continued to deteriorate. Rival factions interfered with UNOSOM operations, firing on unarmed peacekeepers, hijacking vehicles, looting convoys and warehouses, detaining staffs, even shelling ships attempting to deliver supplies to Mogadishu. NGOs, the Organization of African Unity, the League of Arab States, and the U.N. secretary-general appealed to the Bush administration to do something.

President Bush authorized humanitarian relief airlift missions, and on 28 August, Central Command launched Operation Provide Relief to airlift supplies into Somalia from bases in Kenya. Military Sealift Command ships carried the supplies to the airheads. CENTCOM also helped to move a 500-man Pakistani contingent of U.N. peacekeeping forces to Mogadishu from 12 September through 3 October 1992. The *Tarawa* ARG provided tactical command and control of U.S. air operations in that effort and then turned these duties over to the *Tripoli* ARG.

By late fall, it became clear that the food still wasn't getting through. On 3 December 1992, the U.N. Security Council adopted Resolution 794, authorizing military force to help create a secure environment for the delivery of humanitarian aid in Somalia, and asking member nations to participate. President Bush responded to Resolution 794 by launching Operation Restore Hope the next day.

Restore Hope was a peacekeeping mission, not a humanitarian-relief operation. Its commander, Marine Lieutenant General Robert B. Johnston, reported to CINCCENT. General Johnston had the authority to take any military action necessary to accomplish the mission, including the preemptive use of force. The plan involved establishing order, ensuring that the civil relief organizations were functioning, and then turning operations over to the United Task Force, a "blue beret" force of U.N. peacekeepers authorized by Resolution 794.

On 9 December 1992, the amphibious ships *Tripoli*, *Rushmore* (LSD 47), and *Juneau* (LPD 10), with the 15th MEU(SOC) embarked, arrived on station off the Somali capital. That same day, the Marines landed in Mogadishu on a mission to restore order in southern Somalia. The *Ranger* carrier battle group steamed offshore, her air wing ready to respond, if necessary.

An initial force of 2,000 grew into a combined joint task force of more than 40,000 troops from 24 countries—Australia, Belgium, Botswana, Canada, Egypt, France, Germany, Greece, India, Italy, Kuwait, Morocco, New Zealand, Nigeria, Norway, Pakistan, Saudi Arabia, Sweden, Tunisia, Turkey, United Arab Emirates, United Kingdom, United States,

Sailors from the cruiser Vicksburg *(CG 69) return Iranian mariners rescued from their sinking dhow to an Iranian civil authorities patrol craft, 15 August 2004.*

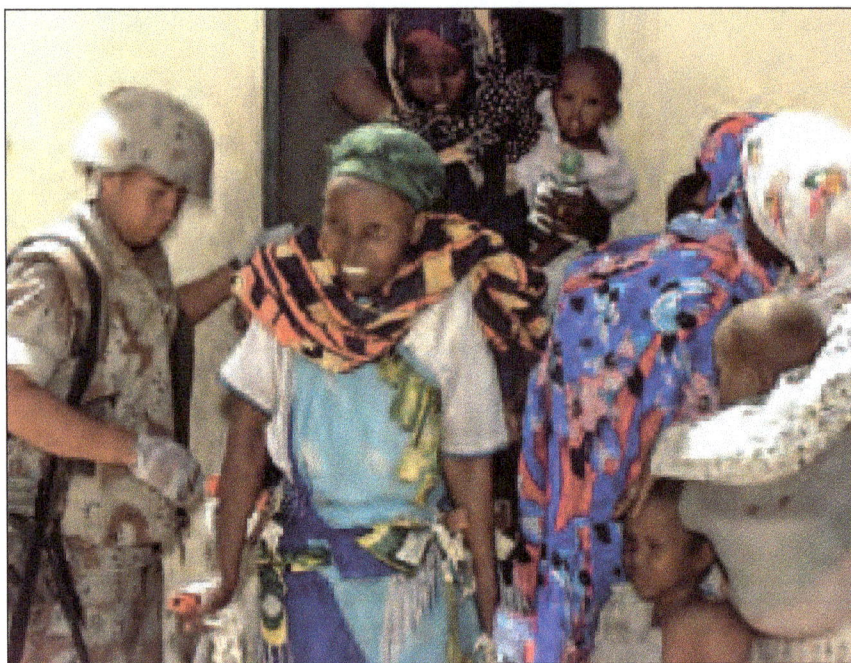

U.S. Marine Corporal Jose Serrano helps a Somali woman at a clinic in Mogadishu, where Navy doctors were conducting a medical civic action mission during Operation Restore Hope, 17 January 1993.

and Zimbabwe. Coalition forces, spearheaded by Marines and the Army's 10th Mountain Division, occupied the major Somali towns that served as distribution centers for the relief groups. As a result of negotiations with the warlords of the 14 principal clans and sub-clans, the militiamen stepped aside to let the coalition do its job.

By the end of December 1992, coalition forces had restored order in southern Somalia. Airlift operations continued while 365,000 tons of cargo and 1,192 containers of supplies were unloaded at seaports and moved safely inland. The provisions mitigated the famine, but not before hundreds of thousands of Somalis had died. The airlift of food and other supplies under Operation Provide Relief continued through February 1993, totaling 2,500 missions flown and 28,000 metric tons delivered.

On 26 March 1993, the United Nations established UNOSOM II to continue peacemaking operations in Somalia under U.N. leadership. Operation Restore Hope ended as UNOSOM II began. On 4 May, General Johnston turned over operations to the UNOSOM II commander, Lieutenant General Cevik Bir of Turkey. By then

most U.S. forces had already been redeployed, but a residual American presence remained to support the U.N. command.

Security in Mogadishu proved short lived. Although General Mohammed Farah Aideed had signed a disarmament agreement, he did not long abide by it. Violence erupted on 5 June, when Somali militia killed 25 Pakistani soldiers in Mogadishu. Other attacks on U.N. troops and facilities followed. In response, UNOSOM II pursued a coercive disarmament program featuring patrols, weapons confiscations, and operations against Aideed's militia and depots.

On 6 June, the Security Council passed Resolution 837 authorizing UNOSOM II to "take all necessary measures against all those responsible" for the previous day's attack. On 22 August, the Secretary of Defense directed the deployment of a joint special operations task force to support U.N. efforts in Somalia. The mission of Task Force Ranger, as it was called, was to capture Aideed and his lieutenants.

On 3 October 1993, Task Force Ranger launched its seventh operation in Mogadishu against Aideed. The task force apprehended 24 suspects, including two of Aideed's key aides. A fierce battle ensued. Somali militiamen shot down two Army Black Hawk helicopters, killed 18 American soldiers, and wounded 75 others, while U.S. forces killed an estimated 1,000 Somalis and wounded between 3,000 and 4,000 more. Immortalized in a book and a movie entitled *Black Hawk Down*, the battle came to symbolize the bravery of the American Soldier as well as the violence of urban combat.

As a result of this incident, on 7 October 1993, President Clinton announced that all U.S. troops would be withdrawn from Somalia by the end of March 1994. Meanwhile, additional U.S. forces were deployed to protect troops already in Somalia, support U.N. operations there, secure lines of communication, and redeploy U.S. forces by the President's deadline. The aircraft carrier *Abraham Lincoln* (CVN 72) arrived that October on station near Mogadishu, as did the *New Orleans* (LPH 1) and *Guadalcanal* (LPH 7) amphibious ready groups with their embarked Marine expeditionary units. All carriers departed by December. Withdrawal of U.S. forces from Somalia was completed on 25 March 1994.

The United Nations, however, kept UNOSOM II in operation for another year, albeit with a reduced troop commitment. In early 1995, the Security Council decided to withdraw U.N. peacekeepers from Somalia by the end of March. Meanwhile, the United Nations brokered further cease-fire agreements among the warring factions in Somalia.

President Clinton committed U.S. forces to assist in the withdrawal, code-named Operation United Shield. Central Command deployed more than 4,000 men and women, supported by five naval combatants, support vessels, and combat support aircraft to conduct the operation. A coalition naval task force, including American, British, French, Italian, Malaysian, and Pakistani ships, stood by off Mogadishu. On 8 February 1995, a Pakistani brigade and a Bangladeshi battalion redeployed from Mogadishu's airport to its seaport. Two weeks later an Egyptian brigade withdrew by air and sea. The final withdrawal began on 28 February, when 1,800 U.S. and 350 Italian Marines landed at the eastern portion of the Mogadishu seaport to secure a lodgment area. These forces provided a rear guard for the departure of the Pakistanis and Bangladeshis, and then completed their own withdrawal on 3 March. Operation United Shield resulted in the safe withdrawal of 6,200 UNOSOM II peacekeepers and 100 combat vehicles without a single casualty or significant damage to equipment.

Ultimately, the U.N. efforts failed to bring lasting political stability to Somalia. Since

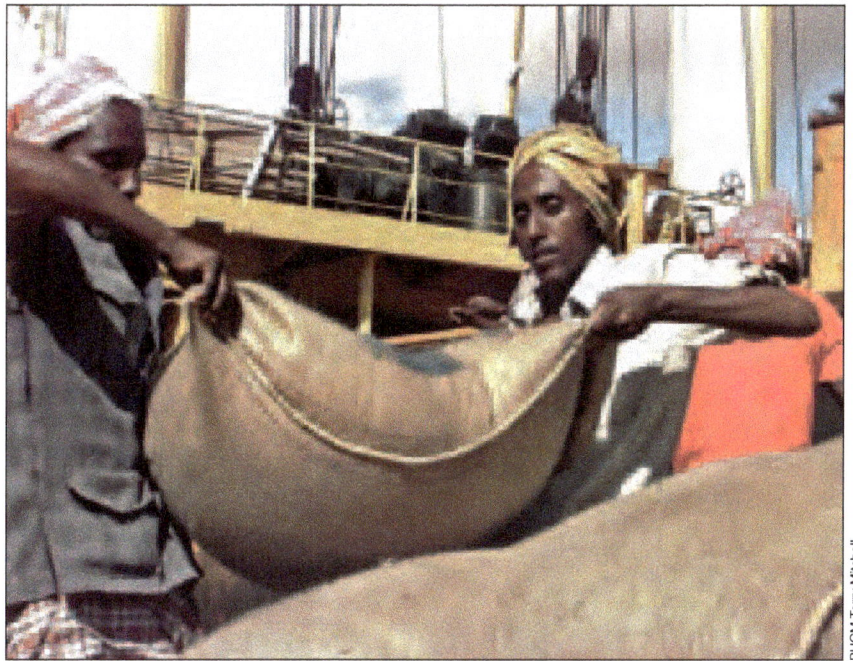

Somali workers at the port of Mogadishu unload a ship carrying sacks of wheat donated by European countries during Operation Restore Hope, 1 December 1993.

UNOSOM II ended, three regions (Somaliland, Puntland, and Jubaland) have declared independence from Somalia, have functioned autonomously, and have attained a degree of peace and prosperity without U.N. help. Rival factions entrenched in different parts of Mogadishu and throughout southern Somalia continue to rule by violence.

America's original purpose in becoming involved in UNOSOM I was to address the massive starvation and illness that resulted from the Somali civil war. The goal of UNOSOM II was to reconstitute a legitimate government in Somalia and then to withdraw peacefully. The support that the international community gave UNOSOM II proved totally inadequate to meeting that goal. Although the U.N. effort failed to rebuild the internal structures of a functioning state in Somalia, the humanitarian relief operations did save tens of thousands of lives.

Whether delivering food and medical care to disaster victims or repairing the engine of a stranded fisherman's dhow, Sailors assigned to Naval Forces Central Command have always answered the call of fellow human beings in need. +++

ENGAGING AMERICA'S ALLIES

THE U.S. NAVY'S ROLE IN THE MIDDLE EAST involves not only fighting and preparing for war but helping our friends prepare for war. Traditionally, Central Command's theater blueprint has included forward presence, security assistance programs, and combined exercises. This cooperative engagement strategy has enabled America to maintain its access to the region, enhance the readiness of its allies, facilitate deterrence, stimulate coalition building, promote stability, and protect U.S. interests. Naval Forces Central Command supported CENTCOM's cooperative engagement strategy by participating in joint and combined naval and military exercises—more than 40 per year after 2001—with members of the Gulf Cooperation Council and other allies and friends, as well as with other U.S. military forces.

In the wake of Desert Storm, American diplomats encouraged the GCC states to improve their defensive capabilities, integrate their defense plans and programs, and involve external powers such as Egypt, Britain, and France. To help achieve these goals, the United States concluded defense agreements with Bahrain and Qatar for weapons sales, training, and combined exercises. The Kuwaiti government signed a 10-year security pact with the United States in September 1991, allowing U.S. forces to preposition military equipment and conduct exercises within Kuwait's borders.

Although the leaders of these Muslim states routinely opposed the permanent basing of Western ground and air forces in their countries, they enthusiastically supported a strong U.S. military presence in the gulf and an increase in multinational cooperation. In November 1993, Colonel Ahmed Yousef al-Mullah, Commander Kuwait Naval Forces, observed that he and other regional naval leaders were concerned about "offensive weapons acquisition programs" being undertaken by "our large non-Gulf Cooperation Council neighbors." "Long-term regional security in the Arabian Gulf," he said, "is vitally dependent on building a strong maritime coalition."

During the 1990s, the U.S. Navy sponsored gulf maritime commanders conferences to discuss a broad range of multilateral activities like maritime interception operations, command post exercises, port visits, development of common operating procedures, sharing of relevant information, and multilateral training programs in areas such as submarine surveillance and antisubmarine warfare.

American policy objectives aimed at improving not only the combat readiness of the region's armed forces but also their ability to operate as part of a team with Western military units. Toward these ends, CENTCOM leaders engaged their commands with the GCC states' naval and air forces in combined military exercises. These exercises improved the coalition's ability to project power, promoted forward presence, honed naval combat skills, and fostered better navy-to-navy relations.

Unlike the huge REFORGER (Return of Forces to Germany) exercises that NATO held in Europe from 1969 to 1988, many of the exercises NAVCENT conducted in the early 1990s were small, bilateral operations involving only a single ship or a handful of aircraft from the participating Arab country. But the U.S. and Arab navies also conducted larger exercises, including special warfare operations, night replenishments at sea, aerial strike operations, amphibious landings, equipment demonstrations, and communications testing. The commander of Destroyer Squadron 50 coordinated the Navy's regional exercise program for surface combatants. Besides improving the combat readiness of GCC military forces and their interoperability with Western forces, the purpose of these exercises included demonstrating both the determination and the growing capability of the GCC states to resist aggression.

In the year before the Gulf War, American and Arab naval forces carried out only two combined exercises in the gulf. But, during Rear Admiral Taylor's tour as COMUSNAVCENT (April 1991–October 1992), they accomplished at least 125, a reflection of the changing nature of the security relationship between the United States and its friends in the CENTCOM region. In 1995 alone, U.S. naval forces in the gulf conducted more than 60 exercises. Some of these exercises were one-time-only events. Others occurred as one in a series of exercises, often conducted annually.

On 3 January 1992, U.S. and Saudi forces launched Red Reef III, the largest bilateral naval exercise in which the Saudi navy had yet participated. The exercise involved almost two weeks of live surface-to-surface and air-to-surface missile firings and amphibious training in the North Arabian Sea and Arabian Gulf. The Royal Saudi Naval Forces, designed for coastal patrol, had never before operated for such a long time on the open sea. The following month, more than 70 U.S. Navy and U.S. Air Force and Royal Saudi Air Force aircraft executed Exercise Indigo Anvil, the largest bilateral evolution in which the Royal Saudi Air Force had participated to that date.

The Native Fury series of exercises, held annually in Kuwait since 1992, tested the global "force-in-readiness" concept. The exercises consisted of practice in unloading maritime prepositioning ships, navigation and aerial strike drills, tests of command

A formation of Egyptian and U.S. Navy aircraft over-fly a pyramid near Cairo during Exercise Bright Star '83. Left to right: Egyptian F-4 Phantom, Egyptian F-16 Falcon, Egyptian Mirage 2000, Navy F-14 Tomcat, Egyptian MiG-21, Egyptian MiG-19, Navy A-7D Corsair II, and Navy A-6E Intruder.

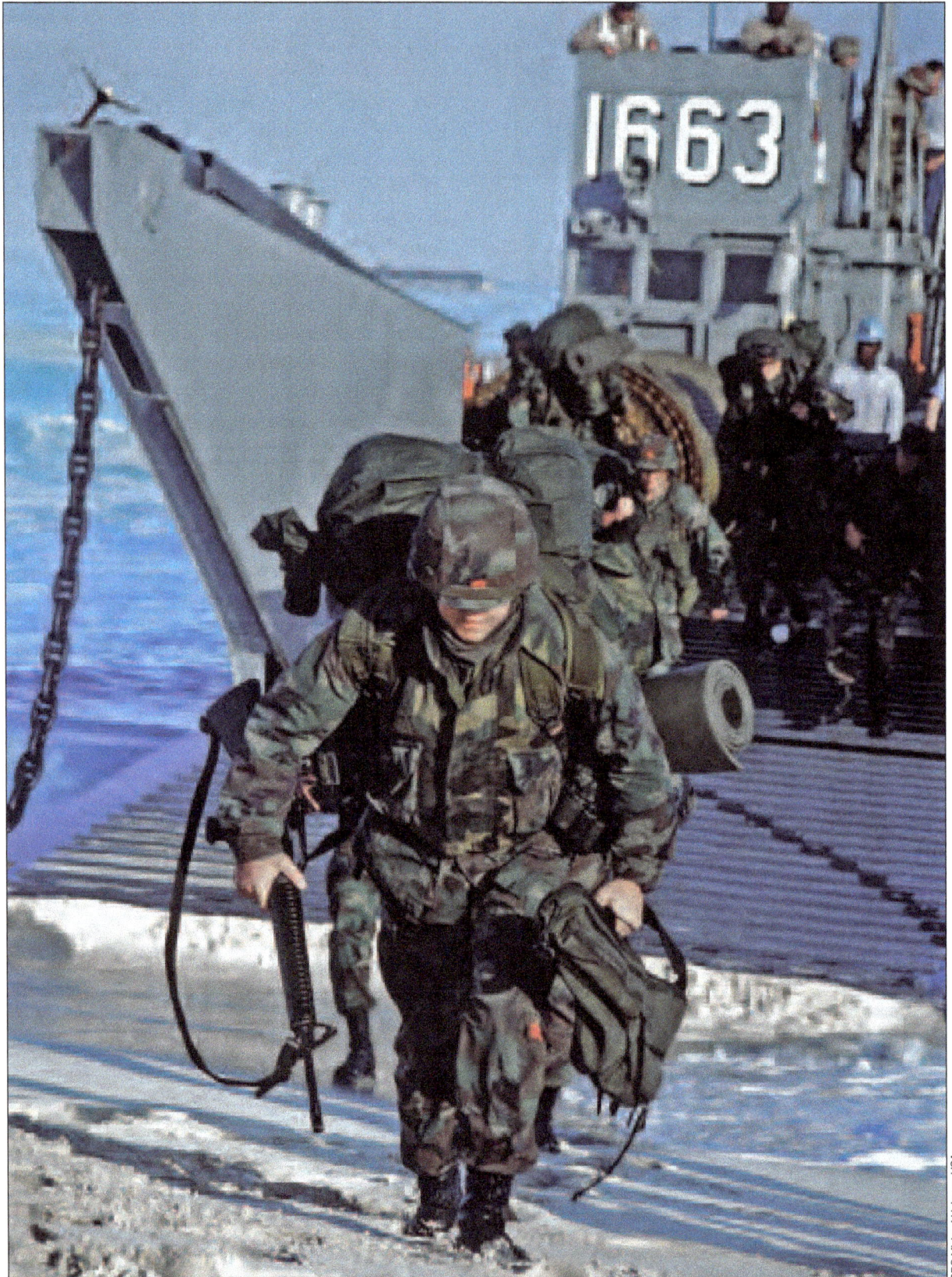

A Seabee steps ashore in Egypt during Exercise Bright Star '94.

and control procedures, intelligence and surveillance training, field training, and command post exercises.

In 1994, Naval Forces Central Command launched the Eager Mace exercise series. Conducted yearly, Eager Mace was a combined amphibious training exercise with the Kuwaiti armed forces, intended to promote interoperability and enhance coordination between Kuwaiti military personnel and U.S. Sailors and Marines. An amphibious ready group and its embarked Marine expeditionary unit typically participated in Eager Mace, which variously consisted of helicopter, air-cushioned landing craft, light armored vehicle, and amphibious assault vehicle operations, as well as ground assault and live-fire exercises. In 2002, the exercise was cut short after terrorists killed one Marine and wounded another in Kuwait.

One of the largest series of exercises was the Bright Star series, conducted every other year in conjunction with the Egyptian government since 1981. In the fall of 1999, Bright Star 99/00 involved

forces from 11 countries and 33 observer nations. Some 70,000 troops took part in this field training exercise, which emphasized interoperability, combined operations, and computer simulation. Bright Star 99/00 featured large-scale maneuver operations and demonstrated CENTCOM's amphibious capabilities. U.S. participation in Bright Star was scaled back in 2001 and cancelled in 2003 because the country assigned needed forces to the Global War on Terrorism (GWOT).

In early 1999, Fifth Fleet Sailors and Marines conducted a bilateral, combined arms training exercise with the armed forces of Kenya. Called Edged Mallet, the exercise was designed to strengthen military-to-military relationships, increase interoperability, familiarize American service men and women with Kenya's environmental and operational characteristics, refine operational readiness of participating forces, and promote understanding between Kenyans and Americans. During the operation, Sailors and

The Bahrain Self Defense Force frigate Sabha *(F 90) steams beside the destroyer* Higgins *(DDG 76) during an exercise in the Arabian Gulf, 30 January 2001. Bahrain acquired this* Oliver Hazard Perry-class *frigate from the U.S. Navy in 1997.*

Electricians Mate Senior Chief Hassan Salem of Bahrain enjoys a photo opportunity with Gas Turbine System Technician (Mechanical) 3rd Class Houston Brooks during a visit to Higgins, *29 January 2001.*

A Saudi Arabian corvette fires a Harpoon antiship missile during Exercise Red Reef III, 10 January 1992.

and Kenyan forces conducted another edition of Exercise Edged Mallet in 2002.

Naval Forces Central Command's participation in combined exercises demonstrated America's commitment to the security and stability of the Middle East, South Asia, and East Africa. While deterrence remained the ultimate goal of

Marines of the amphibious ship *Harpers Ferry* (LSD 49) and 13th MEU(SOC) also distributed 7,000 pounds of humanitarian, educational, and goodwill materials donated by American citizens and businesses to the people of Mombasa. American

CENTCOM's cooperative engagement strategy, preparing to fight as a team with the armed forces of America's allies will enable Central Command to defeat any threat to the region's security in the event of war. +++

CONTAINING IRAQ

I N THE DECADE FOLLOWING THE GULF WAR, containment of Iraq (and Iran) remained the primary strategic consideration in shaping U.S. military planning and force posture for the Middle East, South and Central Asia, and East Africa. During the latter half of the 1990s, containment of Iraq largely meant enforcing the U.N. resolutions passed in the wake of Desert Storm and using force against Iraq when it violated those resolutions. Throughout this period, Naval Forces Central Command enforced the sanctions against Saddam. By the twenty-first century, the number of American warships, officers, and Sailors assigned to these Fifth Fleet operations at times exceeded the size of the forces committed to the Sixth Fleet in the Mediterranean.

Iraq remained Central Command's primary focus during this period. Operation Desert Storm had ended with an U.N. mandate for Iraq to submit to a Special Commission—UNSCOM—that would oversee the elimination of the regime's weapons of mass destruction in return for Iraq's reintegration in the international community and the lifting of economic sanctions.

Between the Gulf War and the end of his time in power, Saddam Hussein focused on one set of objectives—the survival of himself, his regime, and his legacy. To secure these objectives, the Iraqi dictator sought to exploit his country's oil wealth, project the image of a strong military capability to deter internal and external threats, and portray himself as a great Arab leader. He believed that reconstituting Iraqi WMD would enhance both his security and his image.

But to do so, the dictator reasoned, he first needed to end the U.N.-imposed sanctions against Iraq. Saddam considered these sanctions, along with

The destroyer Russell *(DDG 59) fires a Tomahawk during the opening hours of Operation Desert Strike, in which allied forces bombed military targets in response to Iraqi aggression against its own Kurdish population, 4 September 1996.*

the Oil-for-Food Program, as an economic war against his regime, and he regarded Operations Northern Watch and Southern Watch as campaigns of that war. His strategy centered on breaking free of U.N. sanctions and liberating his economy to enable pursuit of his political and personal objectives unfettered. For the rest of his time in power, the Iraqi dictator performed a dangerous high-wire act, seeking to balance the need to cooperate with U.N. inspections—to gain support for lifting sanctions—with his intention to preserve Iraq's intellectual capital for WMD with a minimum of Western intrusiveness and loss of face.

At the same time, Saddam viewed the leaders of the other Arab gulf states as undeserving of the respect the West accorded them. They had done nothing to earn this respect, he believed; the West simply wanted their oil. Saddam especially resented Saudi Arabia, whose leadership of OPEC

On the flight deck of Enterprise, *a Marine Corps F/A-18C Hornet waits in afterburner for the signal to launch during Operation Desert Fox.*

and stature among Arab states in the Western world rankled him. Saddam sought to supplant the Saudi position of leadership in whatever way he could.

During the summer of 1995, Saddam resorted to saber rattling to test American resolve, intimidate his neighbors, and divert Iraqi citizens' attention from their economic woes. That August, the dictator moved a significant Iraqi military force close to his country's border with Kuwait.

Central Command responded by accelerating scheduled military exercises with Kuwait, deploying a second aircraft carrier to the region, and moving Maritime Prepositioning Ship Squadron Two from Diego Garcia to the area of responsibility in Operation Vigilant Sentinel. Through rapid movement of forces to the region, the Navy helped deter Iraqi aggression.

Meanwhile, Iraq's Kurdish population remained restive. Operations Provide Comfort and Northern Watch had created a semi-autonomous Kurdish region in northern Iraq. The city of Irbil, located 48 miles east of Mosul, close to the Turkish and Iranian borders, served as its capital. In March 1996, Kurdish rebels operating from the region launched a failed attempt to topple Saddam. On 31 August, an Iraqi Republican Guard mechanized division, with

support from regular Iraqi army soldiers, attacked and captured Irbil. This renewed Iraqi aggression alarmed the United States and its coalition partners. Saddam threatened GCC members if they assisted the United States, while Iraqi air defense forces launched surface-to-air missiles against U.S. aircraft patrolling the northern and southern no-fly zones.

Central Command responded by planning and executing Operation Desert Strike. On 4 September 1996, the destroyer *Laboon* (DDG 58) of Task Force 50 and B-52 bombers from Barksdale Air Force Base, Louisiana, launched 12 cruise missiles against surface-to-air missile and command and control facilities in southern Iraq. CENTCOM also deployed Air Force fighters, an Army heavy brigade task force, and a second aircraft carrier to the region.

On the diplomatic front, the United States and the United Kingdom expanded the southern no-fly zone from the 32nd to the 33rd parallel and promised a disproportionate response if the Iraqis repaired the damaged air defense sites. The expanded no-fly zone nearly reached southern Baghdad and forced Iraq's air force to relocate all of its tactical aircraft to more northerly bases, thereby reducing the air threat to Kuwait, Saudi Arabia, and coalition aircraft flying in support of Operation Southern Watch.

In the fall and winter of 1997, Saddam rattled his saber once again, violating the no-fly zones, threatening to shoot down reconnaissance aircraft, and interfering with U.N. weapons inspection teams. In February 1998, he denied UNSCOM access to presidential palaces believed to function as weapons depots or factories. That same month, U.N. Secretary-General Kofi Annan traveled to Iraq in person to negotiate with the Iraqi dictator.

To pressure Iraq into compliance with UNSCOM and to bolster the U.N. negotiating position, Central Command on 18 January 1998 launched Operation Desert Thunder, a large-scale deployment of U.S. and coalition forces into the theater. The *George Washington* and *Nimitz* (CVN 68) carrier battle groups had been standing watch in the region since the previous fall. *Independence* relieved *Nimitz* in February and *John C. Stennis* (CVN 74) relieved *George Washington* in March to maintain a two-carrier presence in the gulf until mid-May. These Fifth Fleet forces, combined with coalition ships such as the British carriers *Invincible* (R 05) and *Illustrious* (R 06), comprised a fleet of 50 ships and submarines and 200 naval aircraft, which assembled in a matter of weeks to put weight behind diplomatic efforts. Eventually, Central Command mustered more than 35,000 Soldiers, Sailors, Marines, and Airmen, most of them American. Argentina, Australia, Canada, the Czech Republic, Hungary, New Zealand, Poland, Romania, Slovakia, United Kingdom, and Kuwait rounded out the force by providing liaison teams, aircraft support, special operations elements, base defense units, and medical personnel. This highly visible deployment resulted in short-lived compliance by Iraq with U.N. inspection requirements.

Saddam continued to play cat and mouse with the United Nations. Baghdad stopped cooperating with UNSCOM in August 1998, only permitting the inspections to resume in late November, while denying the inspectors the documents necessary for verification.

The latter action was the last straw. The U.N. withdrew its inspectors from Iraq permanently. On 15 December, UNSCOM Chairman Richard Butler formally declared that verifying Iraq's compliance with U.N. resolutions was not possible given the legacy of Iraqi obstruction.

The next day, Central Command launched Operation Desert Fox, a punitive air campaign against Saddam's regime. For four days, American and British manned aircraft and cruise missiles

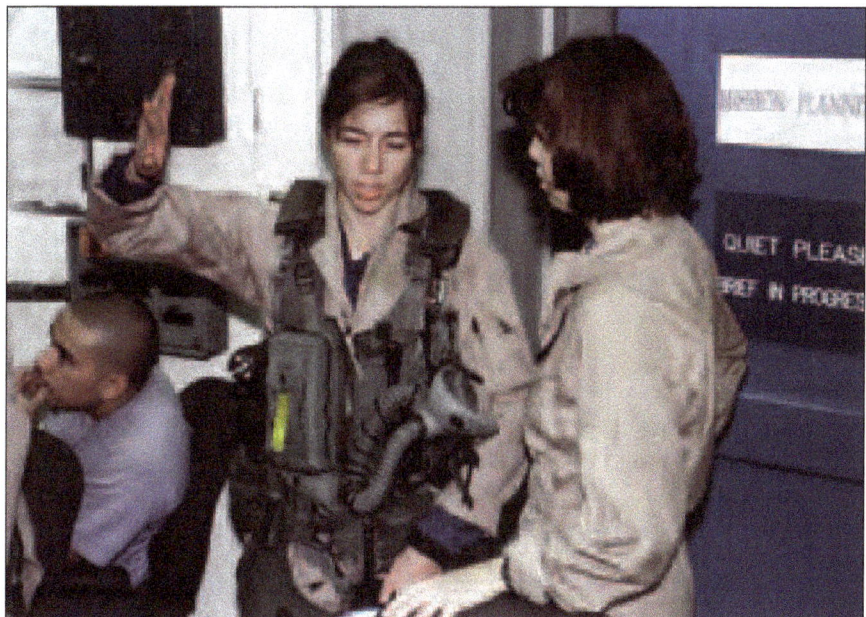

Lieutenant Carol Watts, an F/A-18C pilot, describes a night strike against Iraq on 17 December 1998 during Operation Desert Fox.

struck installations thought to be associated with WMD development, units providing security to such programs, and Iraq's national command and control and air defense networks. Missions targeted television transmitters, Republican Guard barracks, surface-to-air missile sites, missile production centers, airfields, a Basra oil refinery involved in oil smuggling, and L-29 trainer aircraft believed to be undergoing conversion into unmanned aerial vehicles for carrying biological weapons.

After seven days on the ground in support of Operation Desert Fox, these Marines from the 31st Marine Expeditionary Unit will return by air on Christmas morning 1998 to the Belleau Wood *(LHA 3) Amphibious Ready Group.*

CENTCOM estimated that the strikes killed at least 1,600 Republican Guard soldiers. U.S. strike forces included Navy tactical aircraft from the carriers *Enterprise* and *Carl Vinson* (CVN 70) and 325 Tomahawks, as well as Air Force tactical aircraft, bombers, and 90 conventional air-launched cruise missiles. *Carl Vinson* chopped to Fifth Fleet during the operation, while the other ships had already been on station in the region supporting Southern Watch and maritime interception operations. Kuwait and Oman provided access to bases and overflight rights; Bahrain and Saudi Arabia permitted support operations.

In the wake of Desert Fox, Saddam tried harder than ever to bring down a coalition aircraft. According to an Iraqi news report published in January 1999, the dictator offered a $14,000 bounty to any unit that shot down an American or British plane over the no-fly zones and an additional $2,800 reward to anyone who captured a coalition pilot. Between then and 2001, Iraq mounted more than 1,000 antiaircraft artillery attacks, launched 600 rockets, and fired 60 surface-to-air missiles against coalition aircraft.

The United States responded by striking back at Iraq's air defenses. On 27 January 1999, the Clinton administration promulgated rules of engagement that permitted American aircraft patrolling the no-fly zones to target a wider range of Iraqi air defense systems and related installations in an effort to reduce Iraq's overall air defense capability. By early 2001, coalition aviators had entered the southern no-fly zone in Iraq about 153,000 times since the first sortie nearly nine years earlier. Although these missions remained dangerous, they had become so routine that British pilots referred to them as "recreational bombing." The Iraqis failed to bring down a single manned aircraft during this period.

Although these operations weakened Iraq's military infrastructure, Saddam continued to refuse to submit to U.N. inspections, terminating all ties to UNSCOM. Members of the Arab League, as well as Iran, France, Russia, and China, criticized the United States and Britain over the strikes. This criticism represented but one manifestation of a growing erosion of support for the sanctions among certain U.N. members and other nations and played neatly into Saddam's strategy. +++

MARITIME INTERCEPTION OPERATIONS

ALTHOUGH THE DESERT STORM CEASE-FIRE had ended the fighting between coalition and Iraqi forces, coalition navies continued to conduct maritime interception operations (MIO) in the Arabian Gulf against Saddam's regime for more than a decade. Designed to enforce U.N. sanctions imposed on Iraq in the wake of the invasion of Kuwait, these operations cut off the flow of military supplies, equipment, and weapons into Iraq during the Gulf War and hindered Saddam's efforts to rearm.

United Nations Security Council resolutions (UNSCRs) underpinned maritime interception operations in the Arabian Gulf. Resolution 661 (6 August 1990) prohibited export of cargo originating in Iraq and forbade import of cargo into Iraq, except medical supplies and food. Resolution 665 (25 August 1990) called on coalition naval forces to verify compliance with the sanctions.

On 16 August, President Bush directed Central Command to begin enforcing an embargo of Iraqi trade and NAVCENT began maritime interception operations the following day.

The U.N. resolutions resulted in the creation of the Multinational Interception Force (MIF), as coalition countries committed ships and aircraft to ensure compliance with the embargo as well as the

Two members of a boarding team from the destroyer Goldsborough *(DDG 20) disembark from the Iraqi merchant vessel* Zanoobia *after inspecting the ship's cargo, 4 September 1990.*

smooth, efficient flow of legitimate maritime traffic in the Arabian Gulf. Its goals included deterring violation of UNSCRs; facilitating the timely flow of humanitarian goods, imports, and authorized crude oil exports; and minimizing the burden on legitimate commerce. In the absence of a permanent U.N. military organization and staff, the U.S. Navy took the lead in developing a command and control system for MIF operations.

The Multinational Interception Force, however, was truly an international force. Eventually, scores of warships from 21 nations had participated in the MIF: Argentina, Australia, Bahrain, Belgium, Canada, Denmark, France, Greece, Italy, Kuwait, Netherlands, New Zealand, Norway, Oman, Poland, Qatar, Saudi Arabia, Spain, the United Arab Emirates, the United Kingdom, and the United States. The U.S. Navy and Royal Navy had participated continuously since the beginning.

During Desert Shield and Desert Storm, coalition naval forces conducted interception operations in the Arabian Gulf, Gulf of Oman, Gulf of Aden, and Red Sea, paying particular attention to the choke points at the Strait of Hormuz, Bab al-Mandab, and Strait of Tiran. After the Gulf War, the MIF focused on the Northern Arabian Gulf.

UNSCRs passed after Desert Storm also affected maritime interception operations. Resolution 687 (3 April 1991) demanded that Iraq destroy, remove, or render harmless chemical and biological weapons and all ballistic missiles with a range greater than 150 kilometers; forbade Iraq from developing nuclear weapons; demanded that Iraq submit to on-site inspections; and authorized import of food and

Six allied warships assemble in the Gulf of Oman, 6 May 2004.

PH1 Bart Bauer

medical supplies under U.N. supervision. Resolution 986 (14 April 1995) permitted Iraq to use profits from the sale of oil for humanitarian relief, the so-called Oil-for-Food Program.

Resolution 1284 (17 December 1999) removed the cap on oil sales by Iraq under the Oil-for-Food Program and streamlined the application process for a broad range of selected goods. As a result, the amount of Resolution 986 authorized cargo flowing into Iraq increased, and the number of queries and boardings made by the MIF doubled between the years 2000 and 2001. Resolution 1382 (29 November 2001) created a Goods Review List, implemented 30 May 2002, to streamline approval of items under the 986 program.

Throughout this period, the government of Iraq violated U.N. sanctions by supporting the smuggling of oil from its ports. Smugglers purchased oil directly from the Iraqi State Oil Marketing Organization. The illegal sale of oil provided the Iraqi government with quick, untraceable revenue gained outside of U.N. oversight. Saddam Hussein used the profits for purposes other than authorized under Resolution 986. Oil sold to smugglers represented a loss of revenue to the Oil-for-Food Program, but apparently the Iraqi government preferred to sell a ton of fuel oil for $30 hard cash for unregulated use, rather than for $140 for the purchase of food and other 986 authorized goods. Under the 986 program, the only authorized maritime loading of Iraqi oil was at al-Basra Oil Terminal at the mouth of the Khawr Abd Allah (KAA), where the territorial waters of Kuwait, Iraq, and Iran converge in a narrow bight.

Most smugglers obtained oil from the Iraqi government terminal in the KAA, too. After loading the oil, the smugglers would wait in the mouth of the KAA for an opportunity to slip past the Multinational Interception Force. Smugglers used the Shatt-al-Arab for transport of illegal oil loaded at Basra, Iraq, until the Iranians shut the river down in the summer of 2000. Periodically the MIF conducted "MIO surge" operations, focusing on shallow water surveillance, interception, boarding, search, and divert of sanctions violators coming from the KAA.

A P-3 Orion flies a maritime patrol mission on a clear day.

Smugglers took more than 90 percent of the illegal oil to the United Arab Emirates, with Dubai and al-Fujairah the most frequently used destinations. Other destinations included Bandar Abbas in Iran and ports in Pakistan and India. Smugglers brought contraband into Iraq as well. While larger steel-hulled vessels made for UAE facilities almost exclusively, some smaller wooden dhows attempted to skirt coastal waters for destinations in India, Yemen, or the Horn of Africa.

Although smugglers had a 50 percent chance of being caught, they also had a 50 percent chance of making lots of money. The Iraqis sold oil to smugglers at a price 70–80 percent lower than that available in the oil market outside Iraq. A smuggler could make the transit from Iraq to the UAE in several days and realize a profit of five to six times the price he paid for the oil. The run to the UAE did not involve the risks of an open-ocean transit.

Most smugglers had solid ties to the UAE. Although a violation of Resolution 661, UAE terminals accepted illegal Iraqi oil and allowed transfer of Iraqi oil between ships in and adjacent to their territorial waters throughout the 1990s. In June 2001, the Multinational Interception Force began turning over to UAE authorities vessels caught smuggling oil with a traceable tie to UAE citizens. Virtually all of these vessels were in poor or unseaworthy condition. In February 2002, an auction was held in the UAE to sell 28 of these derelict vessels for scrap. At the time, the auction appeared to be a major step towards curtailing the smugglers and demonstrating the resolve of the UAE

On board the destroyer Donald Cook *(DDG 75) in the Red Sea, Ensign Patrick Tamakloe and Lieutenant (jg) Jonathan Keffer record contact with a nearby merchant vessel, 19 March 2003.*

vessel's identity, point of origin, destination, and cargo. MIF ships queried all traffic north of 29° north latitude in the Arabian Gulf. Most vessels were allowed to proceed without further ado. When a suspicious merchantman was directed to stop for boarding, the MIF warship would then dispatch a boarding party to inspect the vessel and its papers. Inspection teams boarded the vessel either by small boat or helicopter. After boarding, the team secured the ship's bridge and engine-room and had the ship go dead in the water. They checked for discrepancies between the ship's crew list and who was actually on board. Vessels needing closer inspection or deemed to be in violation of a U.N. Security Council resolution were diverted to coalition ports. Vessels that refused to stop underwent noncompliant boardings.

Diverting oil smugglers required an ocean of paperwork. The process began with COMUSNAVCENT approval of the divert. Then, an officer from the NAVCENT operations branch would forward an after action report to the U.S. State Department. After these two entities agreed on where to divert the vessel, the State Department would send a message to the American Embassy in the selected country. The embassy, in turn, would send a diplomatic note to that country's ministry of foreign affairs. After examining the evidence, including the results of tests of oil samples sent to the U.S. Customs Laboratory, the Navy Judge Advocate General's office would prepare a formal report and forward it to the American Embassy in that country.

Smugglers employed numerous tactics in attempting to evade the MIF. They tried to use the cover of darkness and changing tides to their advantage. When leaving the KAA they often attempted to run along the edges of Kuwaiti territorial waters or through Iranian territorial waters. Iranian forces, however, either imposed a "fine" on the smugglers they intercepted or escorted them to international waters.

As the MIF gained experience against large, laden steel-hulled vessels, the smugglers developed two tactics for using large vessels to smuggle relatively small oil loads. The first tactic involved hiding relatively small amounts of oil in concealed

government, but unfortunately at least half of the vessels were never scrapped. They returned to the smuggling business, some under new names. Even more disturbing, 26 of the 28 auctioned vessels were sold back to their original owners. The lack of strong action by the UAE government prevented the MIF from achieving complete success in enforcing U.N. sanctions.

Command and control of the MIF usually fell to an American destroyer squadron commander. Royal Navy and Royal Australian Navy officers also took turns as MIF commanders.

In a typical interception, the MIF warship queried the vessel's master by radio, requesting the

A French commando trains in boarding techniques.

or nonstandard tanks. Smugglers tried to hide cargo tanks by removing all topside fittings, figuring that without drawings, a boarding team would not know how many cargo tanks the ship should have and might not discover the hidden tanks. The second tactic involved tankers entering Iraq with empty cargo tanks and near-empty ship's fuel tanks. This move proved especially frustrating, for the MIF could not prevent them from entering Iraq without cargo. When asked about their intentions, these smugglers commonly declared they were going to "have their hull cleaned" or "change out their crew." In Iraq, the smugglers would fill the ships' fuel tanks with far more fuel than was necessary to reach a bunkering port in the Arabian Gulf. Upon departing Iraq, they would claim to be empty, noting their empty cargo tanks. A few ships that carried legitimate, U.N. authorized cargo into Iraq also used this ploy.

Many smugglers were repeat offenders. The MIF documented more than 25 steel-hulled vessels that engaged in Iraqi oil smuggling more than once. Such ships often changed their names or falsified their documents to evade the MIF.

Most smuggling vessels produced false certificates of registry. Many vessels claimed affiliation with flag states that they believed would be difficult to trace, such as Sao Tome, Honduras, Belize, and Georgia. The MIF contacted these countries to validate these claims and, on almost every occasion, the registries turned out to be forgeries. Many of these stateless vessels belonged to smuggling "fleets."

Many repeat offenders operated small dhows. Some oil-laden dhows attempting to exit Iraq were sent back only to return day after day. In many such cases, the Iraqis would not allow the vessels to off-load their contraband cargo. Eventually, however, either the Iraqis would relent and permit the dhows to return the oil, or the MIF would remove the oil from them.

In 1997, a UNSC 661 committee letter (S/AC.25/1997/CC.5560 of 17 December) authorized ferries to operate between ports in Iraq and other

Sailors on a VBSS mission motor two RHIBs through Arabian Gulf chop as they head for a cargo dhow, 13 June 2004.

gulf ports, provided the ferries transported only passengers and personal effects (later modified to include personal vehicles); did not load cargo in Iraq, including fuel; and so forth. Soon, however, smugglers used the ferries to transport contraband goods into Iraq in violation of United Nation sanctions.

The Iraqi government worked hand-in-hand with the smugglers. Increasing intercept rates by the MIF led smugglers to acquire dedicated reconnaissance and intelligence-gathering platforms to monitor MIF movements and activities. The first two reconnaissance vessels noticed by the MIF were "former" Iraqi-flagged fishing trawlers, joined later by a trawler and a former research vessel. Whether run by smugglers or Saddam Hussein's regime, these vessels represented direct support by the Iraqi government to the smuggling network.

Smugglers posed a danger to the environment. To maximize their profits, they kept their costs as low as possible and avoided risking high-value assets. The typical smuggling vessel was 30 years old and in poor condition. Smugglers ignored maintenance of their vessels, disregarded safety equipment, and allowed their state registries to expire. Unregulated and

unmonitored, these stateless vessels became floating hazards. Often loaded in excess of safety standards, they leaked oil or became dangerously unseaworthy, even in calm seas. Several of them foundered. In order to avoid the MIF, smugglers sometimes dumped their oil overboard, polluting coastal waters and fouling beaches in the Arabian Gulf. A significant number of vessels used for smuggling would be banned from major world ports because they presented a potential environmental hazard. Enforcing the existing pollution prevention standards would have prevented many vessels from operating.

Smugglers posed a danger to their own crews. Conditions on board most vessels were awful. Unwilling to fund improvements, owners of smuggling vessels forced ship crews to endure unsanitary, oppressive conditions, compounded by time at sea. Rat and roach infestations were common. During summer months temperatures in interior spaces often exceeded 122 degrees Fahrenheit.

Boarding oil smugglers was a risky business. The poor conditions on most smugglers took a toll on the health of MIF Sailors who boarded several vessels each day. Boarding teams even risked their lives. On 11 November 2001, the MV *Smara* was detained after a boarding party from the destroyer *O'Kane* (DDG 77) discovered oil hidden in her cargo holds. *Smara* was a dry cargo vessel crudely modified to carry liquid cargo. An eight-member security team from the destroyer *Peterson* was posted on board the vessel to keep watch over the 14-man crew. On 17 November, the *Smara* foundered, drowning two American Sailors and four Iraqi crewmen.

The results, however, justified the risks. By curbing outlawed imports and exports, maritime interception operations inhibited Iraqi development of weapons of mass destruction and buildup of conventional warfighting capacity, facilitated the Oil-for-Food Program, and restricted the cash flow directly to Saddam Hussein's regime. As of 18 August 2000, the tenth anniversary of the first maritime interception operation to enforce the U.N. embargo of Iraq, U.S. and coalition naval forces had queried 29,307 merchant ships, boarded 12,763 of them, and diverted 748 to coalition ports for inspection.

Beginning in spring 2001, the MIF increased the pressure on the smugglers. Coalition warships queried more than 2,500 vessels that year. In 2002, the coalition queried nearly double that number. At the same time, illegal loading of oil in Iraq declined 62.3 percent from 2001 to 2002. This drop resulted from the MIF's aggressive tactics. Smugglers that had eluded the MIF before and had returned became trapped in Iraqi waters. Unable to avoid detection, many of these vessels remained in the KAA waterway laden with their illegal cargoes, waiting for any perceived exit opportunity. The size of the average smuggling ship decreased as it became increasingly difficult for large, steel-hulled vessels to evade the MIF. The typical smuggler,

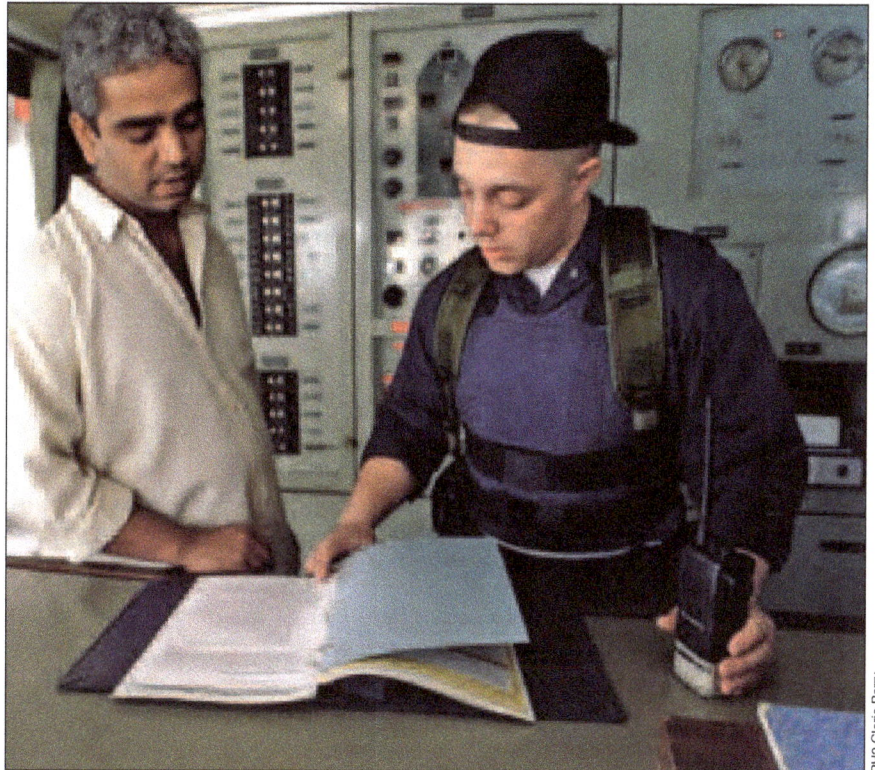

An Iranian ship's master looks on as Lieutenant (j.g.) Vincent C. Watson from the destroyer John S. McCain *(DDG 56) inspects documents during a maritime interception operation in the Arabian Gulf, 6 March 1998.*

therefore, began to load smaller steel-hulled vessel and wooden cargo dhows with oil. Finally, many smugglers left the business, citing their failures at the hands of the MIF. In short, the MIF essentially stopped illegal oil smuggling in the Arabian Gulf.

Before Operation Iraqi Freedom toppled Saddam Hussein's government in March 2003, maritime interception operations were slated to continue as long as U.N. sanctions were in force. Lifting of the embargo was subject to Saddam's compliance with U.N. sanctions. With Saddam Hussein no longer in power, on 16 April 2003, President Bush called upon the United Nations to lift its economic sanctions against Iraq. Three weeks later (7 May 2003), Bush lifted U.S. sanctions on Iraq.

Maritime interception operations constituted an indispensable tool for enforcing sanctions against Iraq both during and after the Gulf War, undermined Saddam's effort to rearm in the wake of Desert Storm, and provided a means for many countries to signal their support for U.N. objectives. +++

A NEW THREAT EMERGES

MEANWHILE, A NEW THREAT TO AMERICA and its allies emerged as virulent Islamic fundamentalism manifested itself in a terrorist organization known as al-Qaeda. In the decade after the Gulf War, this organization mounted increasingly violent attacks on American interests and citizens in CENTCOM's area of responsibility and elsewhere. Naval Forces Central Command was engaged not only in containing Saddam Hussein's regime during this period but also in conducting operations against terrorists.

Much of twenty-first century Islamic terrorism was rooted in the Soviet invasion of Afghanistan, which caused one of the great human upheavals of the late twentieth century. Afghanistan became unstable in the 1970s as both its Communist Party and its Islamic movement grew stronger and became increasingly bitter opponents. In December 1979, Soviet tanks rumbled into Afghanistan in response to a call from the Afghan Communist government for help in a civil war against Mujahidin (holy warriors) insurgents in the countryside. Soviet forces entered the country, occupied the key cities and airfields, and installed their own government. The Soviets intended to prop up the puppet regime, garrison the cities and airfields, establish control in the country, and then withdraw most of their troops within two to three years, after stabilizing Afghanistan's orbit as a Soviet satellite.

Despite modern equipment, air dominance, and overwhelming firepower, however, Soviet leaders soon realized that the job was going to be a lot tougher than they had anticipated. Afghanistan consisted of mountainous desert interspersed with isolated valleys, river basins, and oases, extending eastward from the Iranian plateau and incorporating the foothills of the Himalayas. The Soviet force grew to the equivalent of six divisions, its size limited by what Red Army logistics could support over Afghanistan's primitive and vulnerable road network. By intervening in Afghanistan, Soviet leaders had locked the Red Army into someone else's civil war on some of the most rugged terrain on the planet.

Communist Chinese leader Mao Zedong once said, "The guerrilla must move amongst the people as a fish swims in the sea." The Mujahidin enjoyed popular support, food, and shelter from rural villagers throughout Afghanistan. The Soviets tried to cut off this support by draining the sea—forcing the people from the countryside. Afghanistan's economy rested almost exclusively on subsistence agriculture, with irrigated wheat the major crop. Soviet jets bombed farms, orchards, and irrigation systems that had taken generations of Afghan peasants centuries to establish. Soviet helicopters dropped mines on fields and pastures and machine-gunned livestock. With their means of subsistence destroyed, some 5.5 million of Afghanistan's 17 million people fled to refugee camps in Pakistan and Iran, while another 2 million fled to shantytowns crowded around Afghanistan's cities.

Nevertheless, the Mujahidin fought tenaciously, defending their country against what they perceived as an atheistic ideology, an oppressive government, and a foreign invader. The United States, Britain, France, Saudi Arabia, China, the United Arab Emirates, and other Western and Islamic nations provided aid to the Mujahidin. Pakistan's intelligence service distributed the aid and provided military training to the guerrillas. Non-Afghan Muslims supported the Mujahidin because they saw the Soviet invasion as a war on Islam. Throughout the 1980s, large numbers of Arabs traveled to Afghanistan to join the guerrilla war against an infidel invader. These Middle Eastern guerrillas became known as "Afghan Arabs."

Afghani resistance fighters return to a village destroyed by Soviet forces, 25 March 1986.

One of the most prominent Afghan Arabs was Usama bin Laden, son of a wealthy Saudi Arabian construction magnate. Bin Laden used his personal wealth and connections with rich Arab contributors to finance an entity called the Maktab al-Khidmat, or "Bureau of Services," to facilitate the flow of fighters into Afghanistan. This organization operated a recruiting network in Muslim communities through the Middle East, Southeast Asia, Western Europe, and the United States. Bin Laden provided travel funds and accommodations in Pakistan and training camps and weapons in Afghanistan for the fighters his organization recruited.

The Red Army never gained control of more than 15 percent of Texas-size Afghanistan. Security missions—guarding cities, garrisons, airfields, and lines of communication or escorting convoys—tied down 85 percent of the Soviet force. By late 1985, the Russians realized that they couldn't win the war. They negotiated a settlement and completed their withdrawal in February 1989.

Bin Laden returned to Saudi Arabia a hero. He believed that the subsequent fall of the Soviet Union resulted directly from the Mujahidin victory in what he called the Afghan jihad or "holy war." He discounted the impact of the Cold War on the Soviet economy. He built upon the Maktab to create a new terrorist organization dedicated to waging holy war against infidels around the world. That organization was named al-Qaeda, which, in English, means "the Base" or "the Foundation."

Bin Laden's relations with the Saudi royal family soon deteriorated. When Saddam's forces invaded Kuwait, bin Laden offered to summon Mujahidin to defend Saudi Arabia from possible further Iraqi aggression and to push Iraqi forces out of Kuwait. The Saudi monarchy rebuffed him. Bin Laden considered the American forces that entered Saudi Arabia during Desert Shield as an army of occupation, and he viewed Desert Storm as a war on Islam. When it became clear that a U.S. presence would remain in Saudi Arabia after Desert Storm,

Afghani citizens from the village of Markhanai rest beside a poppy field, 5 May 2002. Soviet destruction of Afghanistan's agricultural infrastructure forced farmers to substitute opium poppies for wheat as the country's principal cash crop.

he declared that the Saudi king had desecrated sacred soil, home to the Mecca and Medina, the holiest sites in Islam. Bin Laden also denounced the royal family for siding with Christians and Jews because of American support for Israel. The royal family, he proclaimed, would have to go the way of the Shah of Iran. Bin Laden left Saudi Arabia in April 1991 and never returned.

Bin Laden lived in Afghanistan until 1992, when he moved to Sudan at the invitation of the fledgling Sudanese Islamic government. He brought resources into Sudan, built roads there, and helped finance the government's war against African Christian separatists in the south. In return, he received permission to establish an operational infrastructure to support terrorism. With al-Qaeda as the foundation, he sought to create an Islamic army that also embraced terrorist groups from Egypt, Libya, Algeria, Saudi Arabia, Oman, Tunisia, Jordan, Iraq, Morocco, Somalia, and Eritrea. Not all groups from these states joined al-Qaeda, but at least one group from each state did.

Bin Laden then set his sights upon the United States. Early in 1992, al-Qaeda issued an edict calling for a jihad against Western "occupation" of the holy lands and singling out U.S. forces for attack. Thereafter, bin Laden delivered an oft-repeated lecture on the need to cut off "the head of the snake."

Over the next several years, bin Laden facilitated terrorist attacks against Americans and American interests in Muslim lands. In December 1992, an explosion outside a hotel in Aden used by American forces as a stopover on their way to Somalia killed an Australian tourist. A Yemeni terrorist group whose leader was close to bin Laden had planted the bomb. In October 1993, when Somali militiamen shot down two Black Hawk helicopters and killed 18 American soldiers, bin Laden's organization had been heavily engaged in supporting the warlords responsible for the attack. On 13 November 1995, a car bomb exploded in Riyadh outside the Office of Program Management of the American-trained Saudi Arabian National Guard, killing five Americans and two Indians. The perpetrators claimed to have

ANCHOR OF RESOLVE

been influenced by bin Laden. On 26 June 1996, an explosion ripped through the Khobar Towers apartment complex housing U.S. Air Force personnel in Dhahran, Saudi Arabia, killing 19 Americans and injuring 372 others. Although a Saudi Shia Hezbollah group had carried out the attack with assistance from Iran, bin Laden was almost certainly involved, according to *The 9/11 Commission Report*. It remains unclear whether the Saudi terrorist played a role in the 1993 bombing of the World Trade Center in New York City or the thwarted 1995 Manila "Bohinka" plot to blow up a dozen U.S. commercial airliners over the Pacific.

Bin Laden wore out his welcome in Sudan by supporting the June 1995 assassination attempt on Egyptian President Hosni Mubarak. Pressure on the Sudanese government from Egypt, Saudi Arabia, Libya, and the United States—all countries targeted by al-Qaeda—made Sudan too hot for bin Laden to remain there. In May 1996, he went back to Afghanistan.

Bin Laden returned to a devastated land. The war with the Soviets had despoiled Afghanistan's countryside, ruined its cities, and killed at least a million of its people. No sooner had the Red Army departed than various Mujahidin factions, once united against a common enemy, began fighting against one another, pitting village against village. Three more years of fighting followed the Soviet withdrawal before the Soviet-backed government fell. Thereafter different groups struggled for control of the capital, Kabul, while the rest of Afghanistan

Mian Khursheed Reuters/Corbis

A Taliban fighter shoulders a machine gun in Kandahar's main bazaar during a visit by foreign journalists, 2 November 2001.

Navy SEALs found this poster of Usama bin Laden in Afghanistan.

area in the Panjshir mountains in the northeast, relative calm prevailed. In others, particularly Kandahar, anarchy reigned.

In 1994, a group of ethnic Pashtun religious extremists, outraged at the behavior of the Mujahidin leaders fighting for power in the Kandahar region, decided to restore law and order themselves. Calling themselves the "Taliban," the Pashtun word for "students of Islam," these fanatics sought to establish a puritanical, medieval form of Islamic law throughout the country. Young people from rural areas and refugee camps on the Pakistan border, disillusioned with the Mujahidin, joined the Taliban as they advanced through southern Afghanistan, imposing their ruthless brand of religious rule by force of arms. The Islamic madrassas in the refugee camps, where Islam was taught by recitation of the Koran, proved fertile ground for recruits. Mullah Muhammad Omar emerged as the leader of the Taliban. By September

functioned as separate fiefdoms, controlled more or less by different Mujahidin leaders. Banditry and extortion flourished, and opium poppies became the principal cash crop. In some places, like the Tajik

Khobar Towers housing complex in Dhahran, Saudi Arabia, after a terrorist bombing killed 19 Americans and wounded hundreds more, 26 June 1996.

George Mulala/Corbis/ SYGMA

Volunteers help a victim a few minutes after an al-Qaeda bomb blast ripped through the U.S. Embassy in Nairobi, Kenya, 7 August 1998.

1996, the Taliban had seized control of Kabul, along with most of the rest of the country. Infamous for edicts banning everything from makeup to kite flying, as well as for punishments including flogging, amputation, and public stoning, the Taliban became one of the most hated regimes in the world. Their draconian rule led to the oppression of women, mass hunger, and the flight of nearly one million refugees.

Bin Laden forged a close alliance with the Taliban. Both espoused a vision of a pure Islamic state. The Saudi terrorist provided significant financial aid to the Afghan fanatics and supplied hundreds, if not thousands of fighters to help them wage war against an alliance of Tajik, Uzbek, and other ethnically based militias in northern Afghanistan, known as the Northern Alliance. Bin Laden's aid

was so extensive that, by the end of the decade, Afghanistan had become a terrorist supported state. In return, the Taliban permitted bin Laden to use Afghanistan as a base and training center to support Islamic insurgencies in Tajikistan, Kashmir, Chechnya, Algeria, Indonesia, and the Philippines.

In August 1996, bin Laden issued a declaration of war against U.S. forces in Saudi Arabia, calling on all Muslims to attack U.S. forces in the desert kingdom. By the end of the year, the U.S. intelligence community had become aware of al-Qaeda's organizational and financial structures, participation in previous attacks, and dedication to attacking the United States. In February 1998, bin Laden and Egyptian terrorist Ayman al-Zawahiri published an edict calling upon Muslims to kill Americans, whether civilian or military, everywhere.

Thereafter bin Laden intensified his campaign of terror against U.S. interests in Muslim lands. On 7 August 1998, massive truck bombs exploded nearly simultaneously outside the U.S. embassies in the East African capitals of Nairobi, Kenya, and Dar es Salaam, Tanzania. The blasts killed more than 200 people, including 12 Americans, and injured thousands of others. Al-Qaeda planned, directed, and executed these attacks under the direct supervision of bin Laden and his chief subordinates.

Almost immediately, Central Command launched Operation Resolute Response, a rescue and recovery effort. Fifth Fleet Sailors and Marines deployed to both countries to locate people still trapped in buildings, treat the injured, airlift those who needed treatment elsewhere, and deal with the Americans who died in the blasts.

On 20 August 1998, Naval Forces Central Command launched Operation Infinite Response, a simultaneous strike against targets in Afghanistan and Sudan in retaliation for the embassy attacks. Five surface warships and submarines launched more than seventy Tomahawk missiles against the Zhawar Kili al-Badr terrorist facilities outside Khost, Afghanistan, near the Pakistan border, where intelligence indicated bin Laden and senior lieutenants would be meeting. Meanwhile, two ships in the Red Sea launched six Tomahawks against the al-Shifa pharmaceutical plant near downtown Khartoum, Sudan, thought to be producing a precursor for the deadly VX nerve gas for al-Qaeda. Both targets sustained heavy damage and at least 11 terrorists were killed, but bin Laden and his principals escaped unharmed before the missiles arrived.

The cruise missile attack did not deter al-Qaeda from mounting further operations against Americans. On 12 October 2000, the destroyer *Cole* (DDG 67) made a brief refueling stop in the harbor of Aden, Yemen, while en route to the Arabian Gulf. The ship had been taking on fuel for less than two

Sailors and Marines patrol past the destroyer Cole *(DDG 67) following the al-Qaeda attack on the ship in Aden, Yemen, 12 October 2000.*

hours when a small boat laden with explosives drew alongside. Witnesses saw two men in the boat raise their hands, and then the boat exploded, ripping a 40-by-40-foot hole in the port side of *Cole*, crushing bulkheads, and peeling back the deck. The blast killed 17 U.S. Sailors and wounded 40 others. For three days, surviving crewmembers fought damage below the waterline that threatened to sink the ship. Their heroic effort saved *Cole* and enabled her to limp home on board the Norwegian transport ship *Blue Marlin* for repairs. The *Cole* bombing was another full-fledged al-Qaeda operation, supervised directly by bin Laden.

In the wake of this attack, Central Command launched Operation Determined Response, a rescue, recovery, force protection, and support effort in Yemen. The frigate *Hawes* (FFG 53), destroyer *Donald Cook* (DDG 75), and tug *Catawba* (T-ATF 168), as well as the amphibious ships *Tarawa*, *Duluth* (LPD 6), and *Anchorage* (LSD 36), converged on the scene to provide assistance and support for the *Cole*'s crew and to stand by to respond to operational taskings. The Air Force furnished airlift aircraft, the Army contributed transportation and medical assistance, and the Marine Corps provided security. Other countries pitched in, too. Yemen provided medical and security support, France and Djibouti helped with initial medical evacuation and treatment, and Royal Navy frigates *Marlborough* and *Cumberland* provided damage control and other assistance. Saudi Arabia, Egypt,

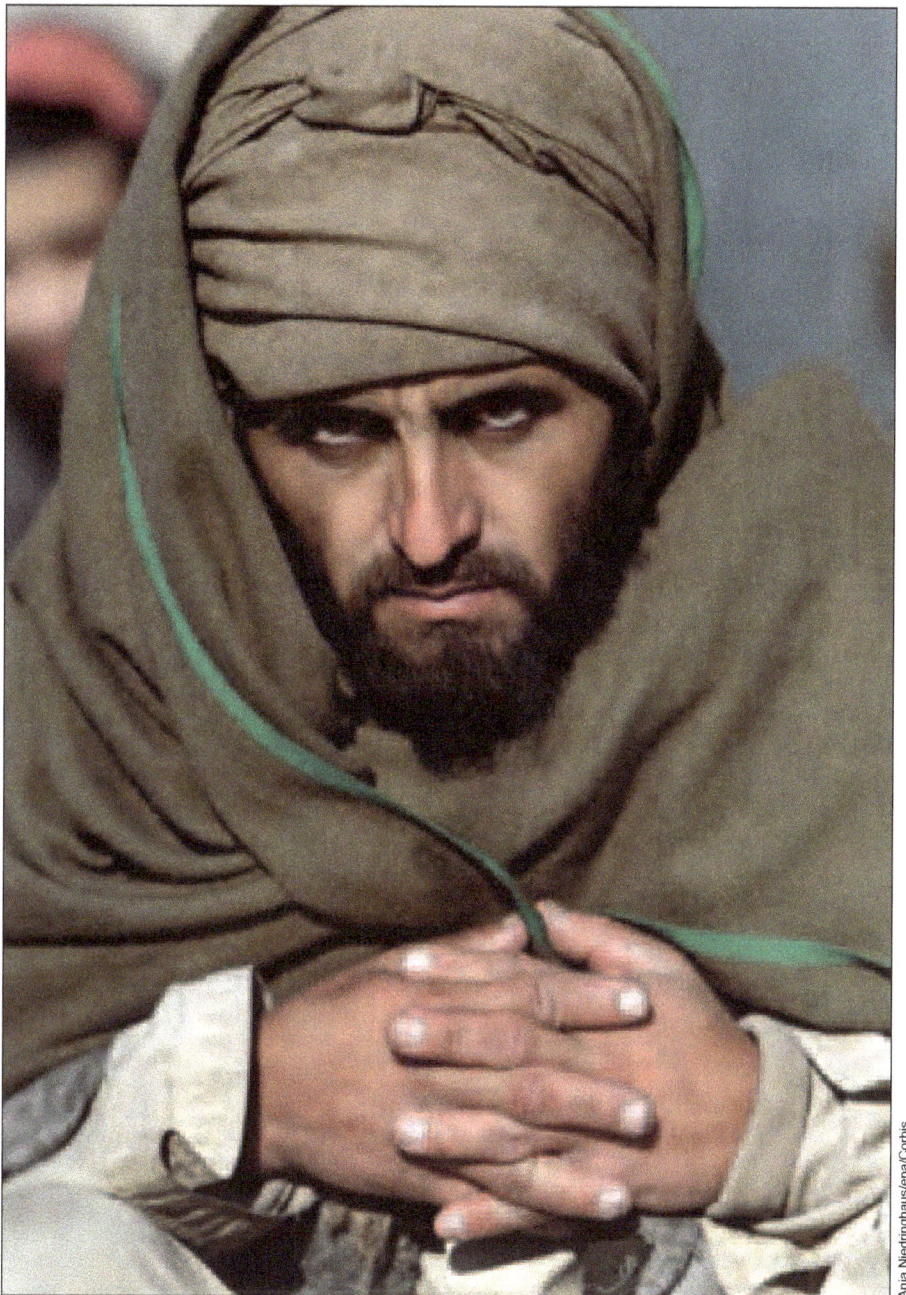

A Taliban prisoner glowers in front of the Red Cross office in Kabul, 10 February 2002.

Anja Niedringhaus/epa/Corbis

Bahrain, Oman, Kuwait, and Qatar granted overflight rights and the use of bases. The Clinton administration failed, however, to respond to the *Cole* attack with military action against al-Qaeda.

In any event, the men and women of Naval Forces Central Command were fighting against the Islamic terrorist threat before many of their fellow Americans knew it even existed. +++

OPERATION ENDURING FREEDOM

BIN LADEN'S NEXT MAJOR ATTACK STRUCK the American homeland and made the whole world aware of the Islamic fundamentalist threat. In response, the United States launched a Global War on Terrorism, conceived as "a new kind of war" involving multifaceted military, intelligence, law enforcement, financial, and cyberspace operations. Operation Enduring Freedom (OEF), the military phase, unfolded mostly in the Central Command theater, mainly in Afghanistan. Naval Forces Central Command played the predominant role in taking the fight to the enemy.

On 11 September 2001, al-Qaeda suicide operatives hijacked four commercial jet airliners and crashed one each into the Pentagon and the twin towers of New York City's World Trade Center. The fourth airliner crashed in a field near Shanksville, Pennsylvania, as passengers overpowered the terrorists. The attacks destroyed the World Trade Center, stove in the southwest side of the Pentagon, and killed nearly 3,000 men, women, and children.

A fireball erupts from the World Trade Center as al-Qaeda hijackers crash United Airlines Flight 175 into the South Tower, 11 September 2001.

Sean Adair/Reuters/Corbis

Half a world away, satellites beamed images of the attacks to the men and women of the *Enterprise* carrier battle group as they were steaming south toward their departure from the CENTCOM area of responsibility near the end of a six-month deployment. Instead of proceeding as scheduled, *Enterprise* came about and made best speed for the North Arabian Sea. Meanwhile, the *Carl Vinson* carrier battle group, slated to relieve *Enterprise* in the AOR, made best speed toward the theater chop line. With the arrival of the carriers, Naval Forces Central Command had 24 U.S. ships, 177 aircraft,

and 18,000 people on station in the North Arabian Sea ready to launch strikes or other combat operations.

In a televised speech to the American people on the evening of 11 September, President Bush characterized the terrorist attacks as "acts of mass murder" and pledged "to find those responsible and bring them to justice." "We will make no distinction between the terrorists who committed these acts," he declared, "and those who harbor them." Dubbed the Bush Doctrine, the latter statement underpinned the strategy for America's Global War on Terrorism.

At that time Central Command had plans for striking al-Qaeda and Taliban targets in Afghanistan with Tomahawk missiles and manned bombers, but no plans for conventional ground operations. Nor had the United States made diplomatic arrangements with Afghanistan's neighbors for basing, staging, overflight, and access rights. Since naval aircraft went to war on board their own bases, naval aviators predominated in air operations over Afghanistan.

Afghanistan.

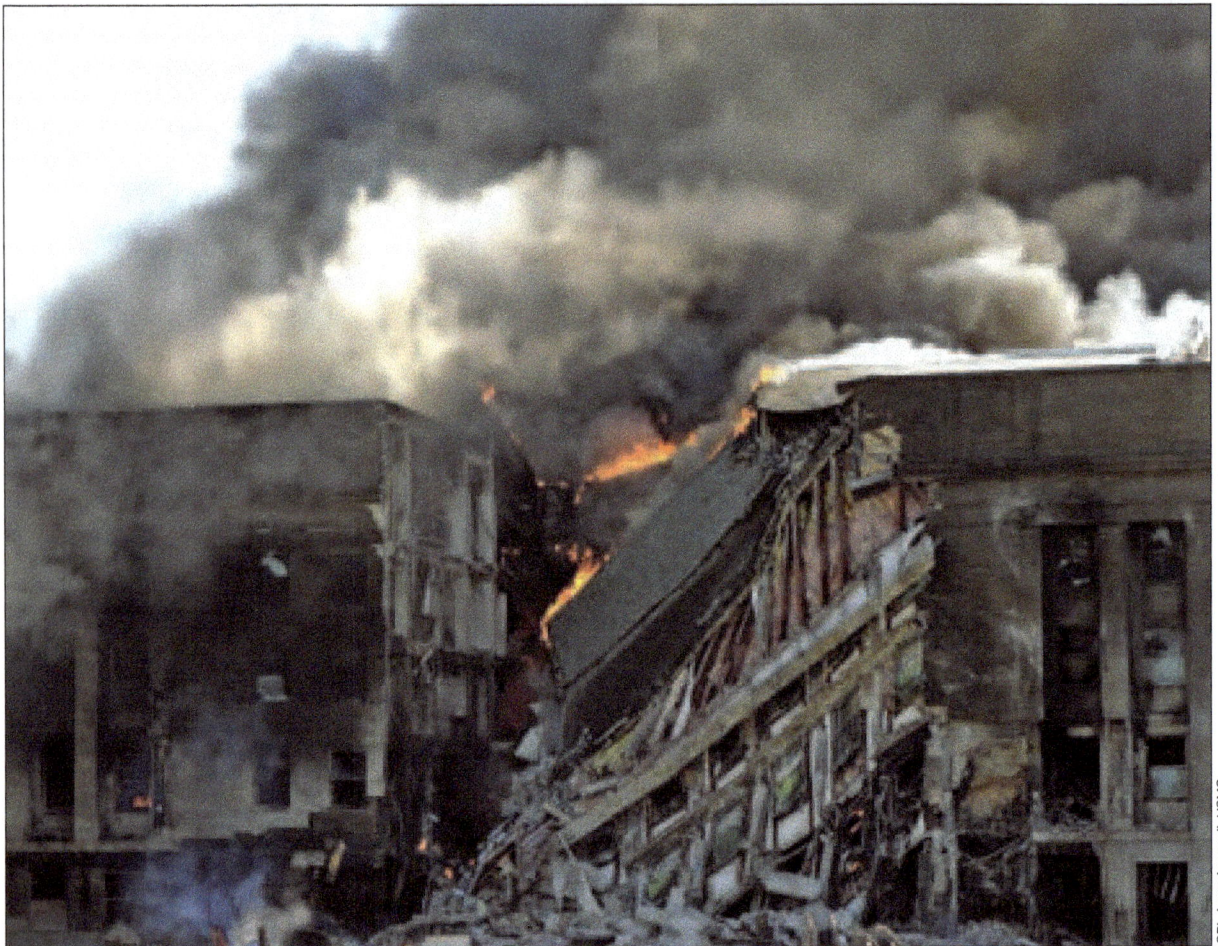

Smoke and flames rise from the Pentagon after hijacked American Airlines Flight 77 slammed into the building, 11 September 2001.

In the absence of an appropriate "off-the-shelf" operations plan, joint planners followed crisis action procedures to formulate and implement Operation Enduring Freedom. During a meeting on 12 September with his war cabinet comprising a half-dozen top officials, President Bush decided to start the war with the perpetrators of the attack and their accomplices and then move on to terrorism in a broader sense. The plan combined air strikes with what planners called "boots on the ground"—small numbers of U.S. troops deployed inside Afghanistan. It called for attaching CIA paramilitary and Special Forces teams to Northern Alliance and anti-Taliban Pashtun units to make U.S. airborne firepower available to them. Army General Tommy R. Franks, Commander in Chief, U.S. Central Command, exercised combatant command from his headquarters in Tampa, Florida.

Taliban forces numbered an estimated 45,000–60,000 fierce but poorly trained and equipped fighters, including bin Laden's Afghan Arabs. By the fall of 2001, they controlled about 90 percent of Afghanistan. The Taliban arsenal consisted mostly of outdated equipment left over from the Soviet era, including approximately 650 tanks and armored vehicles, as many as 100 MiG-21s and MiG-23s, an assortment of armed and utility helicopters, and an unknown number of surface-to-air missiles. One military analyst said that this equipment was so old that it could not be "sustained in combat" and was largely "irrelevant to U.S. forces." Northern Alliance leaders numbered their forces at about 15,000 fighters, and they weren't any better equipped.

After 11 September, however, al-Qaeda and the Taliban faced a far more formidable foe as an unprecedented coalition formed to fight terrorism.

On 12 September, the United Nations Security Council passed Resolution 1368, condemning the terrorist attack. That same day, the North Atlantic Council invoked Article V of the NATO Charter for the first time, thereby considering the attack on the United States as an attack on all member states, and pledged any necessary assistance. Australia and New Zealand also invoked their ANZUS treaty obligations to support the United States. By April 2002, 197 countries and jurisdictions had expressed support for the campaign and its objectives, 136 countries had offered military assistance, 89 had granted over-flight authority, 76 had granted landing rights, and 23 had granted bed-down and basing authority.

Coalition navies participated heavily in OEF. The United Kingdom deployed its largest naval task force since the Gulf War; Italy and France sent their only carrier battle groups to support combat operations in the North Arabian Sea; the Canadian and German navies deployed a high percentage of their naval forces; and Japanese ships delivered fuel to coalition warships. The number of non-U.S. ships steaming in the CENTCOM AOR during Operation Enduring Freedom often exceeded the number of U.S. ships present.

The inherent flexibility of naval forces enabled the U.S. Navy to surge more than three times the number of ships normally assigned to Fifth Fleet without straining organizational relationships, to rotate and relieve forces in place without disrupting operations, and to provide a broad range of warfighting capabilities and support functions. In the first six months of Operation Enduring Freedom, the Navy committed to the theater six aircraft carrier battle groups, four amphibious ready groups, and a total of 60,000 active duty Sailors and Marines plus another 13,000 Reservists. The carrier *Kitty Hawk*, on station in the North Arabian Sea from 12 October to 12 December 2001, served as an afloat forward staging base for special forces. The Navy maintained at least two carriers in the CENTCOM AOR until 18 April 2002. Vice Admiral Charles W. Moore Jr. served as Commander Naval Forces Central Command/Commander Fifth Fleet and Combined Joint Forces Maritime Component Commander until relieved by Vice Admiral Timothy J. Keating in February 2002.

PH1 (AW) Tim Turner

A Navy SEAL covers teammates advancing on a suspected enemy location in Afghanistan, 24 January 2002.

As in previous operations, most of the fuel and ordnance used by U.S. aircraft over Afghanistan came to the region by sea. The Navy's long-standing shore basing at Masirah, Oman, and the British Indian Ocean Territory of Diego Garcia facilitated the deployment of both U.S. Air Force and special operations forces. Besides providing logistic support to the Department of Defense, the Navy defended the sea lines of communication along which supplies flowed.

While U.S. forces surged to the Central Command theater, the U.S. government demanded that the Taliban surrender bin Laden to American authorities. Taliban representatives stated that bin Laden was their guest and had become a resident of Afghanistan before they had taken control. They refused to give him up.

Since the President sought to bring to justice those who harbored terrorists as well as the terrorists themselves, the Taliban's decision meant war. On 7 October 2001, the U.S. Navy, the U.S. Air Force, and allied air forces commenced strike operations against the terrorists and their enablers in Afghanistan and in support of Northern Alliance opposition forces on the ground. Targets included air defense sites, airfields, military command and control centers, and other facilities near major cities and installations.

An F/A-18 pilot from Marine Fighter Attack Squadron 251 carried in his cockpit during one of the first bombing runs against terrorist targets in Afghanistan the Stars and Stripes raised by firefighters over the remains of the World Trade Center in New York, subject of one of the iconic photographs of 11 September. The carrier *Theodore Roosevelt* flew the same flag during subsequent strike operations.

Aircraft carriers and Tomahawk shooters served as force providers to the Combined Forces Air Component Commander (CFACC), who was located at the Combined Air Operations Center (CAOC) at Prince Sultan Air Base, Saudi Arabia. CFACC produced the air tasking order, which included Tomahawk strikes as well as tactical air strikes. Because Air Force fighters lacked access to modern bases in the region, Navy tactical aircraft flew approximately 80 percent of the strike missions over Afghanistan during the war.

Air operations over Afghanistan demanded a high degree of interservice cooperation. The Navy had no heavy bombers and the Air Force had no electronic jamming capability—both key elements in the war. Although the Navy was the majority force provider to the air tasking order run by the Air Force, it could not have conducted its mission

Seabees from Naval Mobile Construction Battalion 133 grade the runways at Camp Rhino, Afghanistan.

An F/A-18C on a mission over Afghanistan.

without Air Force tankers and airborne command and control, and would have been hard pressed to take over the development of the ATO. Navy pilots found Air Force AWACS and tanker crews helpful and professional in supplying fuel. Royal Air Force tankers played an important role as well.

During Desert Storm, the Navy had bristled at top-down control inherent in the JFACC concept, had initially harbored doubts that the ATO system would work, had lacked communications equipment to receive the ATO electronically on the carriers, and had been underrepresented in numbers and rank on the air component staff.

In contrast, Operation Enduring Freedom unfolded with relatively little difficulty between the services. The Navy not only had adapted to the ATO system during Desert Storm but had operated with it for more than ten years afterward while conducting Operation Southern Watch. The Navy had strong senior representation in the CAOC throughout the war. Navy and Air Force tactical aviation, airborne early warning, electronic countermeasures, combat search-and-rescue, tactical recovery of aircraft and personnel, and air logistics systems were fully integrated.

The war shifted rapidly from strikes against preplanned targets to a combination of preplanned and flexible targets. After the first week, naval aviators usually didn't know what targets they would be hitting when they launched. As emerging targets became predominate, the key was to keep aircraft on station over Afghanistan long enough to acquire good targets for their weapons.

To keep up the pace, two carriers typically swung into a day-night rotation. Navy strike fighters averaged two aim points per aircraft per sortie, a significant increase in capability since Desert Storm. A full 93 percent of the Navy strike sorties delivered precision-guided ordnance. Once on station, aircraft became a roving strike force positioned over the battlespace to provide pinpoint firepower on demand. Meanwhile, unmanned aerial vehicles, satellites, and other intelligence sources tracked "time-sensitive targets," particularly Taliban and al-Qaeda officials.

Navy P-3 Orion maritime patrol aircraft proved particularly effective as tactical intelligence platforms. Orions became highly coveted for overland intelligence in support of ground forces as well as for their traditional search mission over water. As

A CH-46 helicopter lands Marines from the 26th Marine Expeditionary Unit on a mountaintop in Afghanistan.

a result, naval aircraft flew the bulk of overland reconnaissance missions during the Afghan war.

Although operational success hinged mainly on the linkage between air and ground forces, the Northern Alliance was not instantly ready for coordinated air and ground offensives. Aid ranging from ammunition to horse fodder had to be flown into the theater and air-dropped to the Northern Alliance forces, while U.S. special operations teams and air controllers had to link up with assigned elements of the Northern Alliance.

Central Command had in place all the pieces needed for rapid success on the ground by late October. With American special operators calling in air support, the Northern Alliance rolled over Taliban and al-Qaeda forces and captured the northern Afghan cities Mazar-e Sharif, Herat, Jalalabad, and Kabul, the capital, by mid-November.

Navy SEALs on horseback with mobile telephone and global positioning system equipment became a characteristic image of the Afghan war. Naval Special Warfare Forces formed the nuclei

of two joint and combined special operations task forces. Combined Joint Special Operations Task Force North, or Task Force Dagger, worked with the Northern Alliance to defeat the Taliban government. Combined Joint Special Operations Task Force South, or Task Force K-Bar, focused on destruction of al-Qaeda's ability to conduct operations in Afghanistan. Together these task forces completed more than 60 special reconnaissance, direct action, and sensitive site exploitation missions; called in nearly 150 air strikes; and destroyed more than half a million pounds of enemy explosives and weapons. A third special operations task force, TF-Sword, operated initially from *Kitty Hawk*.

The swift success of the campaign in the north led General Franks to deploy larger U.S. forces on the ground in the south to complete the destruction of the Taliban and carry the fight directly to al-Qaeda. The 15th MEU(SOC) embarked on board the *Peleliu* ARG and the 26th MEU(SOC) embarked on the *Bataan* (LHD 5) ARG formed the core of the amphibious force for Enduring Freedom. Because

Members of Special Boat Team 12 prepare for a mission in the Gulf of Oman, 21 April 2004. The cruiser Leyte Gulf *(CG 55) appears in the background.*

their mission focused on operations ashore, Vice Admiral Moore chose a Marine Corps general officer, Major General James N. Mattis, as commander of his amphibious forces designated Task Force 58.

To get men and materiel inside Afghanistan, TF-58 Marines established three intermediate staging bases in Pakistan—two inland and one on the beach to allow surface off-load of equipment—for deploying and supplying forces in Afghanistan, refueling aircraft, and regrouping forces on the way out. To provide a base for strikes against Taliban and al-Qaeda elements and a safe haven for Marine forces in Afghanistan, General Mattis established a forward operating base (FOB) at an old desert airfield south of Kandahar, code-named Rhino. The distance between the *Peleliu* ARG and FOB Rhino was more than 400 nautical miles.

The 15th MEU(SOC) began the seizure of Rhino on 25 November 2001. The Marines met no resistance during the initial insertion and completed the buildup of forces there by 3 December 2001.

Two days later, the Marines launched interdiction operations along the main road leading to Kandahar. On the night of 12 December, elements of the 15th MEU(SOC), with assets from the 26th MEU(SOC), secured the Kandahar airfield. Seabees from Naval Mobile Construction Battalion 133 maintained runways and provided other invaluable support to the Marines. The 15th MEU(SOC) began to withdraw from FOB Rhino on 24 December 2001.

From 16 December 2001 through turnover with the 101st Airborne in January 2002, the 26th MEU(SOC) participated in raids of sensitive sites in southern Afghanistan. The 101st Airborne relieved the Marines at Kandahar on 28 January. TF-58 was redeployed to Bahrain on 5 February and disestablished three weeks later as the amphibious command structure in theater returned to its pre-OEF form.

Meanwhile, enemy forces had been reduced to pockets of resistance by mid-December 2001, with some hiding in caves and others on the run. Areas of

U.S. Marines approach an Afghan cave to search for hidden weapons caches, 27 June 2004.

GySgt Keith A. Milks, USMC

strong enemy resistance in eastern Afghanistan, most notably Tora Bora and Zawar Kili, kept coalition and opposition forces busy for the remainder of the month. In 2002, the pattern of operations in Afghanistan shifted from the "hot war" of the previous fall to "presence," punctuated by periods of hot war operations.

On 2 March 2002, coalition forces from Australia, Canada, Denmark, France, Germany, and Norway joined U.S. troops in Operation Anaconda, one of the costliest operations of the war up to that point. Anaconda was designed to assault enemy forces in southeastern Afghanistan. When the operation concluded on 18 March, a total of eight American servicemen had been killed and 82 wounded in action.

In mid-May 2002, General Franks established Combined Joint Task Force 180 to assume responsibilities for the majority of the forces operating in Afghanistan. For the next several years U.S. forces continued searching for al-Qaeda and Taliban remnants and dealt with sporadic outbreaks of violence. Afghanistan remained a dangerous place,

with random sniper or grenade attacks and routine rocket attacks on U.S. bases near the Pakistan border.

At a press conference in Kabul on 1 May 2003, Secretary of Defense Donald Rumsfeld declared that major combat operations in Afghanistan had ended and that U.S. forces there were shifting their focus to stabilizing and rebuilding the country. Rumsfeld noted that small-scale combat operations would continue in Afghanistan against pockets of Taliban and al-Qaeda resistance. The United States committed $1 billion a year in aid to Afghanistan in 2002 and 2003, including $230 million to train and house 9,000 soldiers in a new Afghan army. A functioning Afghan army remained a prerequisite to any withdrawal of U.S. troops.

The United States Navy was crucial to every aspect of Operation Enduring Freedom in Afghanistan. It played the lead role in strike operations, maritime and leadership interdiction by sea, and overland manned tactical surveillance. The Navy also provided key support for the ground war, contributed in significant ways to special operations, and led the OEF maritime coalition. +++

Ships from five nations steam in parade formation during Operation Enduring Freedom, 18 April 2002. From top row left to right: Italian frigate Maestrale *(F 570), French destroyer* De Grasse *(D 612), U.S. carrier* John C. Stennis *(CVN 74), U.S. cruiser* Port Royal *(CG 73), French carrier* Charles De Gaulle *(R 91), British helicopter carrier* Ocean *(L 12), French frigate* Surcouf *(F 711), U.S. carrier* John F. Kennedy *(CV 67), Dutch frigate* Van Amstel *(F 831), and Italian destroyer* Luigi Durand de la Penne *(D 560).*

OPERATION IRAQI FREEDOM

W HILE WAR RAGED IN AFGHANISTAN, U.S. leaders grew increasingly concerned over terrorists getting their hands on weapons of mass destruction, particularly weapons thought to belong to Iraqi dictator Saddam Hussein. The Bush administration concluded that regime change in Iraq was the only way to curb this threat to U.S. national security. When diplomacy failed to persuade Saddam to step down from power peacefully, the United States and a "coalition of the willing" launched Operation Iraqi Freedom (OIF) to topple his regime. The men and women assigned to Naval Forces Central Command were crucial to the success of the operation.

In the days following 11 September 2001, several of President Bush's principal advisors believed that Saddam Hussein was somehow involved in the attacks on America. They debated about whether going after his regime would be an appropriate initial step in the war on terrorism. Bush concluded that he would have to put off the Iraq question until the United States dealt with Afghanistan.

Meanwhile, Saddam was longing for the day when he could uncork the WMD genie again. To make this dream a reality, Saddam tried to get the U.N. sanctions lifted. Since kicking out the U.N. weapons inspectors in 1998, he had managed to make steady progress on the economic, military, Arab relations, and international affairs fronts. By 2001, he had mitigated many of the effects of sanctions and undermined their international support. The increase of illicit revenue from oil smuggling, broadening international sympathy for the humanitarian plight of Iraq's people, and complicity of some of Iraq's neighbors in evading the sanctions led elements within the Baathist regime to boast that U.N. sanctions were slowly eroding. In August 2001, the Iraqi foreign minister declared in an al-Jazeera TV interview that the sanctions had collapsed.

U.S. Marines in amphibious assault vehicles drive up an Iraqi highway through a sandstorm, 24 March 2003.

Sgt Kevin R. Reed

Although the Iraqi dictator had abandoned his nuclear program after the Gulf War, members of his inner circle assumed he would resume nuclear weapons development once the sanctions ended. Beginning in 1992, Baghdad had transferred its former nuclear scientists to related research projects, hoping to retain the intellectual capacity to resume a nuclear program in the future. Throughout the period between Desert Storm and Iraqi Freedom, Saddam took a variety of measures to conceal key elements of the nuclear program, including ordering subordinates to hide and preserve documentation associated with the program from U.N. inspectors.

Saddam also intended to resume a chemical weapons program when the time was right. He believed that the war with Iran had proven such weapons an effective antidote to an enemy's superior numerical strength. But U.N. sanctions had crippled Iraq's chemical weapons program and adversely affected its legitimate chemical industry, which had only begun to recover in the mid 1990s. Thereafter Iraqi chemists conducted a modest amount of dual-use research, which, like the nuclear

Iraq.

An explosive ordnance disposal team inspects ocean mines hidden inside oil barrels on an Iraqi shipping barge captured during the early hours of Operation Iraqi Freedom, 21 March 2003.

weapons program, preserved the knowledge base needed to restart a chemical weapons program. Baghdad apparently harbored no plans, however, for a biological weapons program.

For as long as Saddam had been in power, Iraq had been a state sponsor of terrorism. During the 1970s, Iraq supported Palestinian groups against Israel, including the Palestine Liberation Organization and the Abu Nidal Organization. During the 1980s, Saddam backed off from sponsoring international terrorism so as not to lose assistance from the United States and Western Europe against Iran. During the 1990s, Saddam invited terrorists to Baghdad and provided some of them with weapons and supplies. Iraq also used its own intelligence service in terrorist operations. In 1993, the Iraqi secret service attempted to assassinate Emir of Kuwait Sheikh Jaber al-Ahmed al-Jaber al-Sabah and former President George H.W. Bush. And although Saddam and bin Laden did not develop close ties, they had a common enemy in the United States. U.S. officials feared that Iraq might

someday provide WMD to al-Qaeda or to another terrorist organization.

While no proof emerged that Saddam was involved in 11 September, the Bush administration remained concerned about Iraq's ties to terrorists and alleged WMD programs. In his January 2002 State of the Union address, President Bush named Iraq, along with Iran and North Korea, as part of an "axis of evil." In the National Security Strategy released later that year, Bush said that the United States must work with other nations to "deny, contain, and curtail our enemies' efforts to acquire dangerous technologies," by which he meant weapons of mass destruction. "As a matter of common sense and self-defense," he declared, "America will act against such emerging threats before they are fully formed." This strategy of preemption underpinned Operation Iraqi Freedom.

In the fall of 2002, President Bush began seeking U.N. support for action against Iraq. Administration officials declared Iraq to be in defiance of 17 Security Council resolutions involving WMD. Further delay in taking action against Iraq, they argued, would endanger national security. In October 2002, Congress authorized the President to use the armed forces to defend the country against the Iraqi threat and to enforce all relevant U.N. resolutions regarding Iraq.

In November 2002, the Security Council adopted Resolution 1441, declaring Iraq "in material breach" of U.N. resolutions and giving Saddam a final opportunity to "comply with its disarmament obligations" or "face serious consequences." Iraq accepted the resolution and invited inspectors back into the country that same month. In December, Iraq issued a WMD declaration as required by Resolution 1441. The U.N. Monitoring, Verification, and Inspection Commission judged this document to be incomplete and a rehash of old information.

During January and February 2003, President Bush, other top U.S. officials, and British Prime Minister

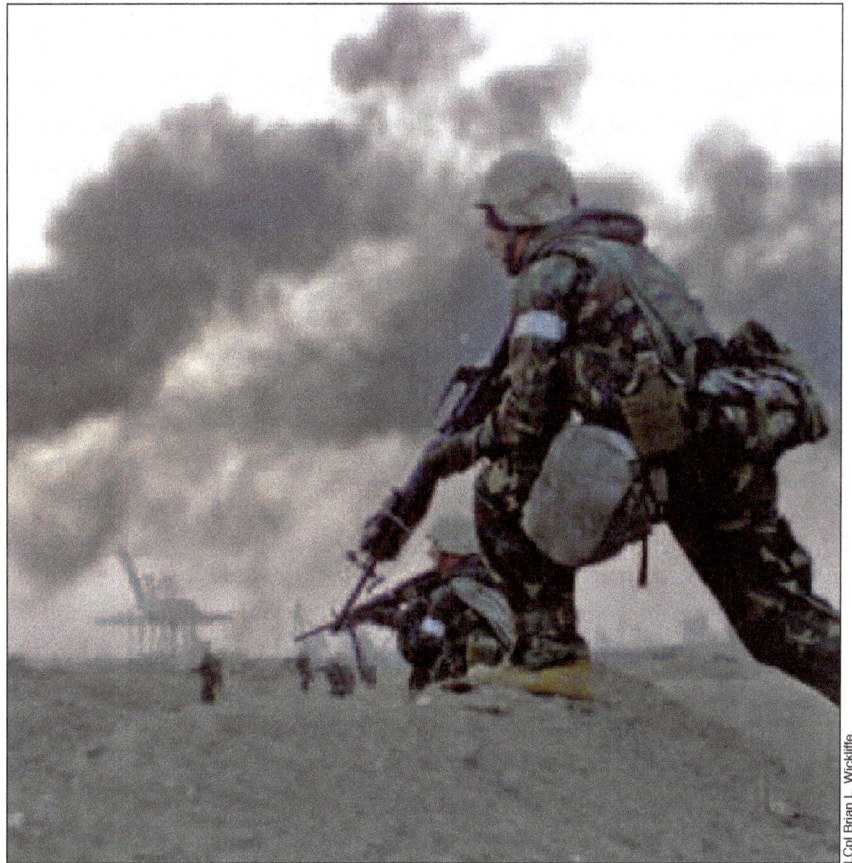

Embodying the timeless image of a combat infantryman, a U.S. Marine charges forward into battle, 23 March 2003.

Sailors from the nuclear attack submarine Toledo *(SSN 769) stand by to receive supplies from* Donald Cook, *27 March 2003.* Toledo *was among the first submarines to launch TLAMs during Operation Iraqi Freedom.*

Tony Blair repeatedly stated that Iraq had little time left to cooperate fully with U.N. weapons inspectors. Leaders of France, Germany, Russia, and China, however, insisted upon giving the inspections process more time.

Meanwhile, Central Command had revamped its operations plan for war against Iraq. The process had begun in November 2001, when Secretary Rumsfeld ordered General Franks to produce a "commander's estimate" of the status of the Iraq war plan. The plan current at the time, described by Franks as "Desert Storm II," had been approved in 1996 and updated in 1998. It premised a six-month buildup of 400,000 people to the theater. Rumsfeld wanted something much faster and leaner.

After many weeks of hard staff work, Central Command completed a new plan to disarm and depose Saddam's regime, code-named Operation Iraqi Freedom. Its centerpiece consisted of a ground offensive in which two main forces—one Army and one Marine—would attack from Kuwait along separate lines of advance and then converge on Baghdad. The Army would advance along a long arc west of the Euphrates River, while the Marines would march farther east along the Tigris River. Meanwhile, a division-plus-size British ground force would pivot northeast out of Kuwait and isolate Basra, securing the southern oil fields. U.S., British, and Australian

Exiled for his role in the uprising against Saddam Hussein's regime after Desert Storm, Khuder al-Emiri (center), a translator for the Marines, reunites with his family after a 12-year absence, 7 April 2003.

SSgt Bryan P. Reed

Special Operations Forces would gain control of Iraq's western desert, denying Saddam the option to launch missiles toward Jordan and Israel. Originally the 4th Infantry Division was to advance into northern Iraq from southern Turkey, but the Turkish parliament made a last-minute decision not to allow coalition forces to invade Iraq from their country.

The coalition faced an Iraqi military about half as strong as it had been during Desert Storm. In 1991, Iraqi ground forces had numbered about 1 million men, 10,800 armored vehicles, and 4,000 artillery pieces. Ten years later, their ground forces numbered about 390,000 men, 6,000 armored vehicles, and 2,400 artillery pieces. Six Republican Guard divisions made up the cream of the Iraqi military. Most other Iraqi soldiers were poorly disciplined, organized, and trained. Iraq's air force fielded fewer than 200 serviceable combat aircraft; its naval force consisted of nine small, outdated combat vessels and unknown numbers of mines and Silkworm land-based antiship missiles.

To fight the Iraqi armed forces, the coalition deployed approximately 290,000 men and women to the region. The major ground formations included the Army's V Corps, the I Marine Expeditionary Force, and the 1 (UK) Armoured Division (Reinforced), which consisted of British Army and Royal Marine forces. These forces fielded about 1,100 armored vehicles and 210 artillery pieces. Coalition air forces supporting OIF peaked at approximately 1,800 aircraft, including 863 Air Force, 408 Navy, 372 Marine Corps, 113 British, 22 Australian, and 3 Canadian aircraft. Fifteen Air Force air wings operated in the region; strategic bombers flew from the British airbase at Diego Garcia and airbases in the Middle East, Europe, and the United States. Coalition naval strength peaked at 176 ships, 115 of which were American. The major combat units assigned to Naval Forces Central Command included five carrier battle groups, two amphibious ready groups, two amphibious task forces, and a British amphibious task group. United Kingdom naval, ground, and air forces numbered more than 47,000 men and women. Australia deployed approximately 2,000 people, primarily

A naval aviator and his wingman enter Iraqi airspace in F/A-18 Hornets, 28 March 2003.

special operations forces. Poland contributed 200 special operations troops.

The OIF plan relied on mobility, speed, precision, and information dominance instead of massive forces to achieve its objectives. It featured rapid maneuver by ground forces across a large operating area to keep the enemy off balance; air and naval forces supported the main advance and struck strategic targets.

Sealift made execution of the plan possible. From January through April 2003, Military Sealift Command moved almost 21 million square feet of war-fighting cargo and equipment and more than 261 million gallons of fuel for the Army, Marine Corps, and Air Force units involved in Operation Iraqi Freedom. At the same time, MSC ships pumped more than 117 million gallons of ship and aircraft fuel and transferred 5.3 million square feet of food, spare parts, equipment, and munitions to Navy combat ships around the world. Altogether, Military Sealift Command moved more than one-third of a billion gallons of fuel and nearly 26 million square feet of war-fighting supplies and equipment in four months.

On 17 March, President Bush issued an ultimatum demanding that Saddam Hussein and his sons leave Iraq within 48 hours. Otherwise, Bush declared in a televised speech to the American people, there would be "military conflict, commenced at the time of our own choosing." Saddam chose not to step down peacefully.

On 19 March, six U.S. cruisers, destroyers, and submarines launched Tomahawks and Air Force aircraft dropped bombs in an attack on a bunker in Dora Farms, a residential compound south of Baghdad where intelligence had indicated Saddam and top lieutenants were meeting. Known as the "decapitation strike," this was an attack on a target of opportunity, not an early start to the air campaign. The dictator survived.

Saddam expected Iraqi Freedom to repeat the pattern of Desert Storm, with a massive, weeks-long air campaign preceding the ground assault. He believed the interim would give him time to gather international support to end the war, torch oil fields, dump oil into the gulf, and dig in his ground forces. The Turkish government's decision not to allow U.S. forces to attack from Turkey reinforced Saddam's belief that a ground war was far off. As a result, Iraqi formations were placed to suppress a rebellion, not to repel an invasion. Saddam didn't believe that coalition forces would get as far as Baghdad, whenever the ground attack began. It was his last major strategic miscalculation.

Coalition forces mounted the OIF air and ground campaigns simultaneously. The initial objectives involved securing the Rumaila oil fields, the oil industry infrastructure in the al-Faw Peninsula, and the al-Basra and Khor al-Amaya oil terminals (ABOT and KAAOT). The Rumaila oil field, located north of Kuwait and west of Basra, remained one of the world's greatest petroleum deposits. Oil wells, gas-oil separation plants, and refineries studded the flat, desert terrain. Pipelines and pumping stations on the al-Faw Peninsula fed the offshore terminals, Iraq's only loading points for tankers. ABOT alone could pump 1.6 million barrels of oil per day and maintained a standing volume of .8 million barrels when not filling tankers.

If the Iraqis torched the wells and opened the pipeline into the Arabian Gulf as they did in Kuwait during Desert Storm, the world would face the greatest oil pollution catastrophe ever. A single day's discharge from ABOT alone would have

been 12 times greater than the total spilled from the supertanker *Exxon Valdez*. Such an ecological catastrophe would hamper efforts to locate and neutralize floating contact mines, interfere with plans to bring humanitarian assistance into Iraq through the port of Umm Qasr, and cripple the desalination plants along the shores of the Arabian Gulf upon which the people of the region depended for water.

After dark on 20 March, five SEAL platoons and one Polish special forces platoon from the Naval Special Warfare Task Group swept in on board helicopters and boats, seized the offshore terminals, and secured the shore-based metering station and pipeline valves that fed oil to the terminals. They accomplished their mission in less than 40 minutes.

That same night, British Royal Marines launched an amphibious assault on the al-Faw Peninsula, with one Australian and three British frigates providing naval gunfire support. Meanwhile, I MEF and 1 (UK) Armoured Division thrust north from Kuwait towards Basra, as SEALs, elements of the 15th MEU(SOC), and 3 Commando Brigade Royal Marines assaulted the port of Umm Qasr. SEALs also

PH1 Arlo K. Abrahamson

The coastal minehunter Cardinal *(MHC 60) returns to Naval Support Activity Bahrain after 45 days at sea conducting mine clearing operations in the Northern Arabian Gulf, 24 April 2003.*

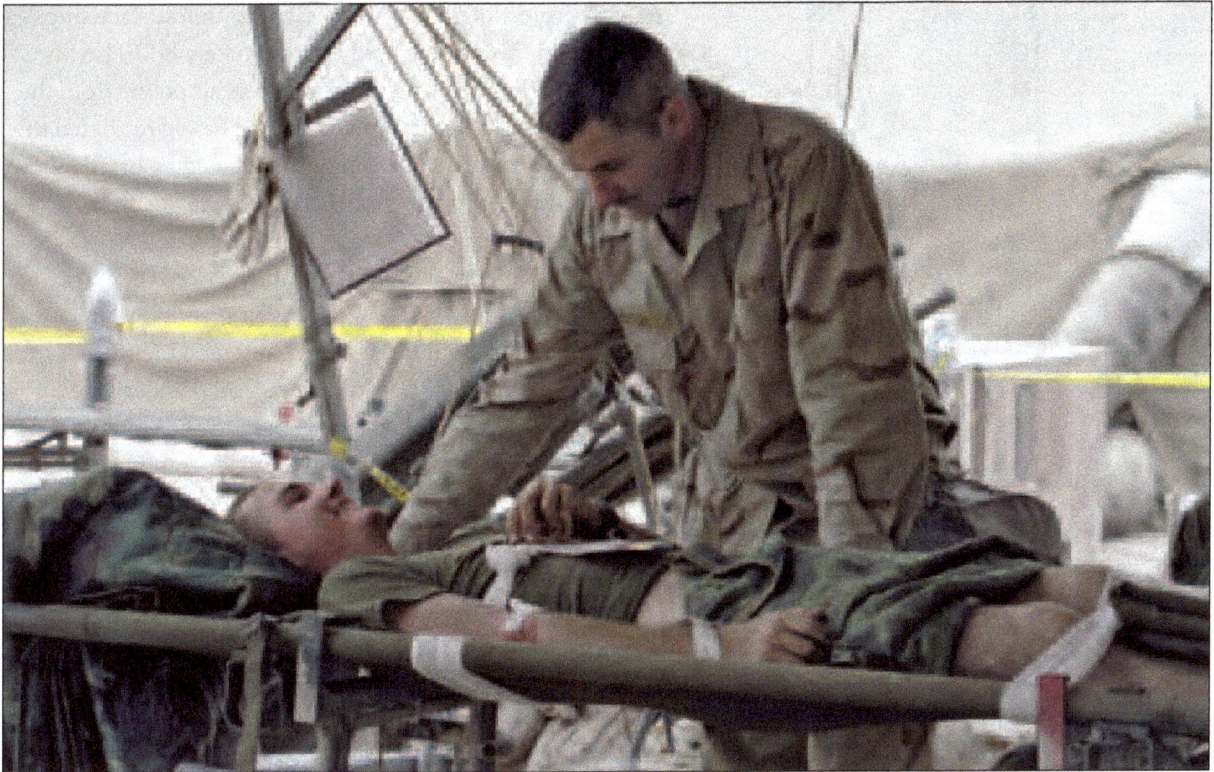

Navy Chaplain Lieutenant Commander John Denton visits Marine Corporal Marco Chavez at Fleet Hospital Three in southern Iraq, 8 April 2003.

assisted British troops in safeguarding the waterways leading to Basra.

By late in the afternoon of 21 March, British and American forces had secured the entire oil industry infrastructure on the al-Faw Peninsula and in the Rumaila fields. Although the Iraqis had booby-trapped these facilities extensively, coalition forces captured them intact and began clearing the demolition charges. The simultaneous start of the ground and air campaigns surprised the Iraqis and averted an oil spill of unprecedented scope.

Coalition naval forces began patrolling Umm Qasr and the associated waterways that same day. American, Australian, and British Sailors captured a number of cleverly disguised Iraqi minelayers in the Khawr Abd Allah waterway before the vessels could sow their mines. Meanwhile, U.S., U.K., and Australian minesweeping and EOD teams commenced operations that enabled provision of humanitarian aid through the port of Umm Qasr by the end of the month. British ground forces entered Basra on 6 April.

Although the OIF air campaign officially kicked off on 21 March, coalition forces had been waging aerial warfare against Iraq since the early 1990s while conducting Operations Northern Watch and Southern Watch. Although Iraq had stopped shooting at aircraft engaged in no-fly-zone patrol missions after the 9/11 terrorist attacks, they resumed doing so two months later. In 2002, Iraq fired upon coalition aircraft about 500 times. At the peak of these attacks, Iraqi forces fired more than a dozen missiles and rockets per day.

Central Command responded by mounting an air campaign against Iraq's air defense network in the southern no-fly zone called Operation Southern Focus. Between June 2002 and March 2003, coalition aircraft struck nearly 400 targets in Iraq. The pace increased during the first 20 days of March, as coalition pilots flew 4,000 strike and support sorties in the no-fly zones, knocking out radars, air defense guns, and fiber-optic links. This effort to "shape the battlefield" was equivalent to Phase II of Desert Storm, "Suppression of Enemy

U.S. Marines prepare to enter one of Saddam Hussein's palaces in Baghdad, 9 April 2003.

Air Defenses." Southern Focus cleared the air route to Baghdad of opposition, allowing initial OIF aerial efforts to concentrate on establishing air supremacy over all of Iraq and attacking strategic targets.

On OIF's first night, coalition air forces saturated the skies over Iraq with more than 1,700 sorties, including 504 Tomahawks and conventional air-launched cruise missiles. Air operations during the first four days focused on strategic targets, including bunkers and presidential palaces in and around Baghdad; national command, control, and communications systems; and facilities associated with WMD. Dubbed "shock and awe" by planners and symbolized by televised images of multiple explosions lighting up the Baghdad skyline, this part of the campaign aimed at paralyzing Iraq's leadership.

After a large shamal or sandstorm blasted Iraq on 24–27 March, the focus of air operations shifted to tactical targets, largely Republican Guard and other Iraqi ground forces south of Baghdad, in support of coalition ground forces. Ultimately, air support of land operations accounted for some 80 percent of the coalition air component's effort.

The Navy began the war with two carrier battle groups operating from the eastern Mediterranean and two from the Northern Arabian Gulf. Another carrier arrived in the gulf after the shooting started. Naval aviation flew 65 percent of the power

projection sorties, while 35 coalition surface ships and submarines fired approximately 800 TLAMs.

The Navy's ability to project air power from the sea proved critical, since limited basing restricted the number of tactical aircraft that could be based ashore. Of the approximately 650 fixed-wing tactical aircraft in theater, just under half were sea-based.

Operation Iraqi Freedom featured the most successfully integrated joint air operations in American military history. Air Force Lieutenant General T. Michael Moseley, Commander U.S. Central Command Air Forces, led the combined forces air component, directing operations from the Combined Air Operations Center. Rear Admiral David C. Nichols Jr., Commander Naval Strike and Air Warfare Center at Naval Air Station Fallon, Nevada, served as General Moseley's deputy during OIF's major combat operations, and a large Navy liaison element represented carrier aviation in the CAOC. Integrated coalition intelligence, surveillance, and reconnaissance systems provided data to the Air Force and Navy air component staff members, who developed the ATO jointly with minimal inter-service difficulties.

OIF air operations showcased many of the fruits of "transformation," broadly defined as the adoption and integration of new technologies, organizational structures, and business practices throughout the Department of Defense during the Bush administration. Instead of large numbers of unguided munitions, U.S. forces used a relative handful of precision-guided munitions to destroy critical targets. Guided munitions accounted for 68 percent of the bombs dropped during major combat operations. If the question during Desert Storm had been how many sorties would it take to destroy a given target, the question during Iraqi Freedom became how many targets could be destroyed in a given sortie. This economy of force enabled the practice of "effects-based" bombing, which entailed using precision air power to produce effects rather than simply to maximize physical damage. Instead of Iraq's infrastructure, coalition air forces targeted power, communications, and fuel supplies to Iraq military forces. Integration of Air Force, Navy, and other coalition intelligence, surveillance, and reconnaissance systems gave Central Command a better picture of Iraqi forces than Iraqi leaders had themselves. The flexibility of the command and control system allowed the CAOC to reassign airborne aircraft to targets that emerged after the aircraft had taken off. All told, coalition air forces delivered about 20,000 strikes, 15,800 of which were directed against Iraqi ground forces, 1,800 against the Iraqi government, 1,400 against the Iraqi air force and air defense targets, and 800 against suspected WMD sites.

U.S. forces benefited from unprecedented situational awareness through a common operational picture provided by a new system called the Blue Force Tracker. Some V Corps and I MEF vehicles were equipped with transponders that automatically reported their positions as they maneuvered across the battlefield, greatly reducing the potential for blue-on-blue engagements.

The two-pronged thrust by Marine and Army forces drove more than halfway to Baghdad in the first five days. By the evening of 24 March, elements of V Corps had reached Karbala, 50 miles from the capital, while I MEF had captured key bridges over the Euphrates River and Saddam Canal at An Nasiriyah. Soldiers and Marines bypassed numerous population centers and military formations along the way, relying on air power to secure their lines of communication. Iraqi forces fought ferociously at times but inflicted few casualties on the coalition and generally died where they stood.

The shamal roared in during the night of 24–25 March. The Iraqis attempted to maneuver their forces under the cover of this "mother of all sandstorms" to parry the Marine and Army thrusts. Coalition aircraft, however, could "see" through the cloud cover, rainsqualls, and blowing sand and dust and pummeled Iraqi armor in the open and troops

Navy Master Diver David Daniels and two Kuwaiti counterparts surface during a debris-clearing operation in Kuwait, 15 April 2003.

A precision strike takes out an insurgent stronghold in Fallujah, Iraq, 10 November 2004.

remaining in defensive positions. The weather cleared on 27 March, revealing the devastation wreaked by one of the fiercest and most effective aerial bombardments in military history.

During the shamal, coalition ground forces slowed their tempo of operations to consolidate supply lines, allow the bombing to do its work, and address the threat from Iraqi paramilitaries known as the Fedayeen Saddam. Founded by Saddam's son Uday in 1995, these "Men of Sacrifice" comprised 30,000 to 40,000 young thugs whose duties included torturing and murdering domestic enemies of the regime. Although U.S. leaders knew the Fedayeen existed, they had underestimated their potential to conduct guerrilla operations. Thousands of Fedayeen had taken up positions in Nasiriyah and other southern cities, determined to put down any Shiite rebellion and to repel the invaders. The Fedayeen not only engaged combat units in fierce firefights but also ambushed convoys. Militiamen from other Iraqi groups and other Islamic countries also participated in guerrilla operations. Many of these irregulars continued fighting after major combat operations ended.

In northern Iraq, coalition forces mounted operations similar to those conducted in Afghanistan during OEF. Instead of a big armored thrust as originally planned, the coalition used scaled-down ground forces to support operations against Iraqi troops by Kurdish guerrillas, collectively known as Peshmerga. About two-fifths of Iraq's conventional forces, stiffened with two Republican Guard divisions, Fedayeen Saddam, and Baath Party militia, were arrayed along the border of the semi-autonomous Kurdish zone. On 26 March, Army paratroopers landed in Bashur, augmenting the special operations forces that had entered northern Iraq four days earlier. Other conventional Army, U.S. Marine, and British special forces units soon arrived. Peshmerga militiamen and coalition forces attacked terrorist training camps along the Iranian border, fought Iraqi troops near Kirkuk and Mosul, and prevented Iraqi formations arrayed in the north from moving against Marine and Army units advancing on Baghdad from the south. Support by carrier and land-based aircraft proved just as crucial to the Peshmerga in Kurdish Iraq as it had been to the Northern Alliance in Afghanistan. SEALs and other special forces operated in western Iraq as well.

On 3 April, elements of V Corps fought their way into Saddam International Airport outside Baghdad. Two days later, Army forces conducted the first of two armored raids into Baghdad, named "thunder runs" for Vietnam War armored reconnaissance-in-force missions into urban areas.

The Marines advanced up the central Mesopotamian valley and, on 3 April, fought one of the war's fiercest battles at al-Aziziyah, halfway between al-Kut and Baghdad. Five days later, elements of I MEF crossed the Diyala River, seized the Rasheed military airfield, and entered the Iraqi capital from the east.

Navy Seabees facilitated the Marines' advance. More than 3,000 Seabees along with 1,000 Marine and Army engineers served under the I Marine Expeditionary Force Engineer Group (I MEG) in Kuwait and Iraq during Iraqi Freedom. A command element and three task forces made up the MEG. Task Force Mike (Mobility) moved forward directly behind Marine combat units and built and maintained bridges, roadways, and airfields. Task Force Charlie (Construction) followed in trace of Task Force Mike, upgrading and maintaining roads and convoying bridging materials, culverts, construction items, food, water, and other materials to forward units. Task Force Echo (Endurance) followed the others, repairing battle damage to infrastructure and preparing for long-term postwar projects. Task Force Echo's first civil-military operation started before major hostilities ended, as a Seabee detachment helped to restore Umm Qasr's electrical power and to develop a system for water purification and distribution.

All coherent enemy resistance in Baghdad collapsed on 9 April and people turned out in the streets in droves to celebrate the fall of Saddam Hussein. Televised images of a Marine tank retriever helping civilians tear down a statue of the dictator in Firdos Square symbolized the Iraqi people's hope for a better tomorrow. The next day Kurdish Peshmerga fighters seized the city of Kirkuk, while Iraqi forces outside Mosul surrendered. Tikrit fell to the Marines on 14 April. Although pockets of Iraqi and foreign resistance remained in many urban areas, coalition forces had gained relative control of all major cities. On 1 May 2003, President Bush delivered a speech on the flight deck of the carrier *Abraham Lincoln*, announcing the end of major combat operations in Iraq.

The United States Navy contributed decisively to the success of the joint and combined team in facilitating the introduction of democracy in Iraq. Naval aircraft flew 65 percent of the power projection sorties during major combat operations. Naval surface and special operations forces averted a potentially unprecedented environmental catastrophe. Naval mine countermeasures and EOD forces cleared the way for shiploads of humanitarian relief supplies. Seabees helped pave the way for the Marines' drive to Baghdad. And Military Sealift Command ships delivered the supplies and equipment necessary to topple the Baathist regime. +++

PHC Tom Daily

Operation Iraqi Freedom marked the first time that six large deck amphibious ships from the East and West coasts deployed together for one war. Led by the flagship Tarawa *(LHA 1), the ships in the second row from bottom to top are* Saipan *(LHA 2) and* Kearsarge *(LHD 3); and in the third row,* Boxer *(LHD 4),* Bataan *(LHD 5), and* Bonhomme Richard *(LHD 6), 20 April 2003.*

GLOBAL WAR ON TERRORISM: CONTINUING THE COMMITMENT

NAVAL FORCES CENTRAL COMMAND continued operations in Afghanistan and Iraq after the major combat phases had ended. The Navy also conducted combat operations, civil affairs missions, maritime interception operations, humanitarian aid, and combined exercises in support of the Global War on Terrorism elsewhere in the Central Command theater. In short, NAVCENT continued to do the same sorts of things it has always done in the Middle East, South Asia, and East Africa.

As Northern Alliance forces swept through Afghanistan in late 2001, U.S. leaders thought that if Taliban and al-Qaeda leaders reached a Pakistani port, they might try to escape by sea. As a result, in November 2001, Naval Forces Central Command broadened the scope of maritime interception operations in its area of responsibility to include visit, board, search, and seizure (VBSS) patrols in the North Arabian Sea and off the Horn of Africa. Named leadership interception operations (LIO) and later called Operation Enduring Freedom maritime interception operations (OEF MIO), the early effort focused mainly on ships transiting the Arabian Sea from Pakistan.

Because al-Qaeda had been so active in the Horn of Africa during the 1990s, U.S. leaders considered the region a likely destination for terrorists fleeing from Afghanistan. In the fall of 2001, Naval Forces Central Command began intelligence, surveillance, and reconnaissance operations in the Red Sea, Gulf of Aden, and western Indian Ocean.

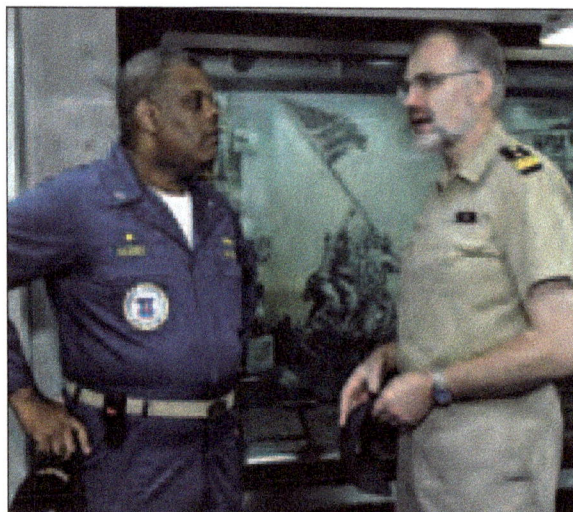

U.S. Navy Captain Sinclair Harris, Commander Amphibious Squadron Four, and German Rear Admiral Heinrich Lange, Commander Combined Task Force 150, discuss the World War II battle for Iwo Jima during Lange's visit to the amphibious ship Iwo Jima (LHD 7), 2 September 2006.

On 3 February 2002, COMUSNAVCENT established Combined Task Force (CTF) 150 to deny the sea to terrorists by countering the illegal movement of weaponry, people, and other materials. Its operating area included the Red Sea, Gulf of Aden, Horn of Africa, and Somalia Basin, as well as the Arabian Sea, Gulf of Oman, and Strait of Hormuz, covering more than 2.4 million square miles of ocean and 6,000 miles of coastline bordering 12 countries. To accomplish its mission, CTF-150 maintained a constant U.S. and coalition maritime presence in these areas, and ships assigned to Naval Forces Central Command began conducting interception operations there.

Commanded at first by an American naval officer, CTF-150 operated thereafter under coalition flag officers. Australia, Canada, France, Germany, Italy, Netherlands, New Zealand, Pakistan, Portugal, Spain, Turkey, the United Kingdom, and the United States contributed ships and aircraft to the task force.

In July 2002, LIO and OEF MIO became expanded maritime interception operations (EMIO) when President Bush authorized European Command as well as Central Command to interdict terrorists and their resources at sea. In 2003, the President approved EMIO to interdict terrorists and their resources globally. Interdiction became a significant mission for every deployed battle group, especially along maritime transit lanes and choke points. These operations resulted in lower insurance premiums in the shipping industry and fewer crimes at sea.

The changing acronyms notwithstanding, the typical CTF-150 mission involved monitoring, inspecting, boarding, and stopping suspect ships and dhows. These operations sought to gather intelligence, inhibit terrorism, and curb piracy, armed robbery, illegal immigration, drug trafficking, and other illegal activity. Between the beginning of Operation Enduring Freedom and the summer of 2005, CTF-150 boarded nearly 1,500 ships within its area of responsibility.

CTF-150 conducted humanitarian operations too. In April 2004, the German frigate *Augsburg*

(F 213) airlifted a crewman with appendicitis from an Iranian dhow and provided immediate medical treatment. In January 2005, the guided missile cruiser *Bunker Hill* (CG 52) rescued a mariner suffering from a life-threatening illness on a Japanese-owned tanker in the Gulf of Oman. In March 2005, the U.S. Coast Guard Cutter *Munro* (WHEC 724), working with the British warships *Invincible* (R 05) and *Nottingham* (D 91), intercepted a hijacked Thai fishing vessel in the Gulf of Aden. CTF-150 ships also conducted exercises with regional nations such as Yemen, Oman, Bahrain, and the United Arab Emirates. And after earthquakes devastated Pakistan in October 2005, the dock landing ship *Pearl Harbor* (LSD 52) took a break from searching vessels at sea to deliver nearly 300 tons of heavy equipment and relief supplies to the port city of Karachi.

In October 2002, Central Command established Combined Joint Task Force Horn of Africa (CJTF-HOA) to combat terrorism in the "the total airspace and land areas out to the high-water mark of Kenya, Somalia, Ethiopia, Sudan, Eritrea, Djibouti, and

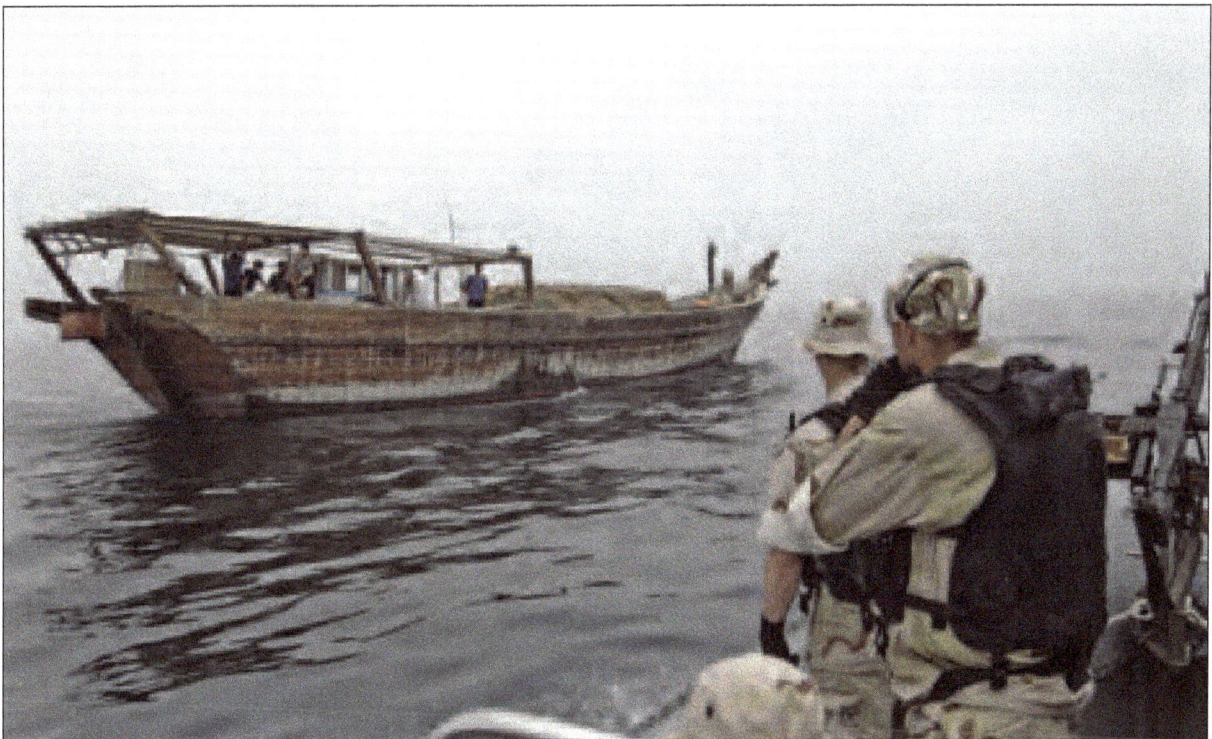

A visit, board, search, and seizure team from the destroyer Bulkeley *(DDG 84) approaches a dhow, 23 April 2004.*

Yemen." Its mission included defeating terrorists, denying terrorists access to the region, and facilitating stability there. Combined Task Force 150 became, in part, the maritime component of CJTF-HOA.

The command ship *Mount Whitney* (LCC 20), operating in the Gulf of Aden, served as the CJTF-HOA headquarters from December 2002 to May 2003, when the staff moved ashore into Camp Lemonier, an 88-acre former French Foreign Legion post owned by the government of Djibouti. The staff included approximately 2,000 U.S. military, U.S. civilian, and coalition force members.

CJTF-HOA spent most of its time training with other coalition forces and selected units from Djibouti, Kenya, and Ethiopia in counterterrorism and counterinsurgency tactics. The task force also conducted a variety of civil affairs missions such as

rebuilding schools and medical clinics and providing medical services.

In Afghanistan, U.S. forces went through six major troop rotations between the fall of 2001 and the spring 2005. On 31 May 2002, Central Command stood up Combined Joint Task Force 180 to assume control of operations in Afghanistan. In February 2005, approximately 18,000 American troops were serving in and around the country, with six coalition nations providing another 1,600 troops. U.S. Special Forces, including SEALs, had operated in Afghanistan since the beginning of the war, and their primary mission remained capturing or killing Taliban and al-Qaeda members.

After Secretary Rumsfeld declared the end of major combat operations on 1 May 2003, Taliban and al-Qaeda remnants continued to conduct

A utility landing craft and an MH-60S Seahawk helicopter answer a distress call off the coast of Kenya, 31 January 2006. Naval forces gave the crew a 10-day supply of food and water to tide them over until a tugboat could tow their disabled ship into port.

PH2 Michael Sandberg

Naval aviators head toward a P-3C Orion aircraft to embark on a mission over the Arabian Gulf, 22 October 2002.

guerrilla warfare against the Afghan government, with occasional attacks against coalition forces, while U.S. forces mounted combat operations to root them out. In March 2005, Joint Chiefs of Staff Chairman General Richard Myers said that the insurgency appeared to be weakening.

According to an April 2005 Congressional Research Service report, Afghanistan's stabilization was gaining strength. Since the defeat of the Taliban, the country no longer served as a safe base of operations for al-Qaeda. Afghan citizens were enjoying new personal freedoms that were forbidden under the Taliban, and women were participating in economic and political life. In January 2004, the Afghan government adopted a new constitution. The following October, the Afghan people turned out in large numbers in what many international observers reported was a "free and fair" presidential election, resulting in victory for Hamid Karzai. The election

went off with minimal violence and a new cabinet was sworn in on 27 December. President Karzai cited the militias controlled by regional leaders as the principal threat to his country's stability, greater than that posed by continuing Taliban attacks. Growing trafficking in narcotics also became a major challenge in Afghanistan. Most observers agreed that a significant U.S. military presence would remain there until the Afghan government became self-sufficient.

The major challenges in Iraq included establishing a democratic political structure, quelling an insurgency, and training sufficient Iraqi forces to assume responsibility for their country's security. The Bush administration asserted that establishing a democracy in Iraq would seed democracy throughout the Middle East and prevent Iraq from becoming a terrorist haven and breeding ground. In May 2003, the administration set up a U.S.-led Coalition Provisional Authority (CPA)

Navy explosive ordnance disposal (EOD) technicians work with Army counterparts to prepare unexploded ordnance for safe demolition near Baghdad, 11 October 2003. Joint Army-Navy EOD teams destroyed munitions throughout Iraq to reduce the amount available to insurgents.

United States handed over sovereignty to this interim government and dissolved the CPA. On 30 January 2005, Iraq held national elections for a transitional national assembly, 18 provincial councils, and the Kurdish regional assembly.

Bush administration officials had expected the process of establishing democracy in Iraq to go relatively smoothly, but a Sunni Arab-led insurgency of unexpected intensity took them by surprise. In July 2003, Army General John Abizaid, the newly appointed CENTCOM commander, said that the United States faced a "classic guerrilla war" in Iraq. After U.S. forces captured Saddam Hussein in December 2003, U.S. commanders said the United States had "turned the corner" against the resistance, but nine months later Secretary Rumsfeld said that the insurgency was "worsening." One observer, writing in August 2005, described what was happening in Iraq as a "multidimensional conflict" including "international terrorism," "banditry," and "civil war."

The insurgency comprised several disparate groups. According to October 2004 CENTCOM estimates, insurgent ranks included approximately 10,000 "former regime elements" (mostly Baathists), 1,000 foreign fighters, 5,000 criminals and religious extremists, and 3,000 Shiite fighters led by radical cleric Moktada al-Sadr. Some Iraqi officials estimated the number of active insurgents to be as high as 40,000, with another 150,000 people playing supporting roles. U.S. officials believed that the insurgency was coordinated loosely at the regional level, but not at the national level.

Insurgent operations sought to drive away international workers, diplomats, and peacekeeping

to govern Iraq. The following July, the head of the CPA appointed a 25-member Iraq Governing Council that had the power to nominate ministry heads, recommend policies, and draft an interim constitution, but did not have sovereignty. The council dissolved on 1 June 2004 when an Iraqi interim government was named. On 28 June, the

ANCHOR OF RESOLVE

Seabee Carlos Hernandez supervises an Iraqi worker near Fallujah, Iraq, 19 May 2004. Seabees taught Iraqis construction skills to help them rebuild their communities.

Sailors assigned to Naval Small Craft Instruction and Technical Training School at Stennis Space Center in Mississippi train members of the Iraqi riverine police force in special boat maneuvers and weapons handling, 23 October 2006.

Tankers load oil at al-Basra Oil Terminal, 12 December 2004. Defending Iraq's gulf oil platforms was one of the Navy's most important missions in support of Operation Iraqi Freedom.

Seabees patrol the streets of Fallujah on 29 January 2005, one day before Iraq's historic democratic elections.

forces; minimize turnout in elections; impede reconstruction; dissuade Iraqis from joining government forces; and provoke civil conflict among Iraq's various groups. The insurgents targeted coalition forces; Iraqi officials, security forces, and civilians working for U.S. authorities; foreign contractors; and oil industry, water, and other infrastructure facilities. Insurgent tactics included ambush, murder, kidnapping, beheading, planting of roadside improvised explosive devices (IEDs), and suicide bombings. A brief lull in attacks followed the January 2005 elections, but afterward the attacks resumed and then worsened considerably during the second half of 2006.

U.S. and Iraqi forces periodically launched offensives against the insurgents, particularly those in Iraq's al-Anbar province, especially in the city of Fallujah, with U.S. carrier aircraft flying in support. Between May 2003 and July 2005, approximately 1,600 Americans were killed in Iraq, 1,350 of them by hostile action.

In June 2003, Combined Joint Task Force 7 stood up to assume operational control of all coalition forces within Iraq. Central Command deactivated the task force in May 2004, replacing it with Multinational Corps Iraq and Multinational Force Iraq because of concern that a combined joint task force headquarters was not sufficient to handle the military workload in Iraq. Multinational Corps Iraq focused on tactical operations, while Multinational Force Iraq focused on strategic aspects like training, equipping, and fielding Iraqi Security Forces.

U.S. forces in Iraq went through three major troop rotations between the beginning of OIF and the summer of 2005. The initial invasion force came to be called OIF-1. The first postwar occupation force, referred to as OIF-2, began deploying in January 2004. The United States began implementing another troop rotation, OIF-3, in July 2004, with the goal being to send new active and reserve forces into the theater for up to 12-month tours of duty. Units of the fourth rotation, OIF-4, began deploying in the summer of 2005. That July, approximately 140,000 U.S. troops were serving in

Iraq, along with 23,000 troops from 27 coalition countries. U.S. leaders planned to keep forces in Iraq until the Iraqi government became capable of securing the country on its own.

Naval forces proved instrumental in supporting the coalition's goals of establishing security and stability in Iraq. Since the end of major combat operations, the Navy maintained a presence of one carrier strike group (CSG) and one expeditionary strike group (ESG) in the Central Command area, while the Marines kept one expeditionary force and three expeditionary units there. The CSG and ESG concepts arose as a result of the Global War

An Iraqi citizen drops his vote into a ballet box during the election for the new Iraqi constitution, 15 October 2005.

on Terrorism. The former was centered on aircraft carriers and the latter on amphibious ships, in both cases combined with other types of warships. Expeditionary Strike Group One, led by *Peleliu*, was the first ESG to deploy overseas, arriving in the CENTCOM area of responsibility in September 2003.

Naval forces maintained a significant presence in Iraqi waters in support of Resolution 1483, passed by the U.N. Security Council on 22 May 2003. Under this resolution, coalition forces provided law enforcement and security functions for the area until an Iraqi maritime security force stood up. By thwarting smuggling and other forms of illegal activity, naval forces helped commercial shipping return to normal in Iraq. Toward these ends coalition naval forces queried more than 6,000 vessels, boarded close to 3,500, diverted approximately 430, and returned to the Iraqi people approximately 60,000 barrels of fuel by the end of 2006. Resolution 1483 also lifted the U.N. sanctions against Iraq.

The U.S. Coast Guard Cutter Baranof *(WPB 1318) passes a fishing dhow while patrolling the waters just off Iraq's Khor al-Amaya Oil Terminal, 7 May 2003. As it had in Operation Desert Storm, the Coast Guard deployed port security units, law enforcement detachments, and patrol boats to the Middle East to support Operation Iraqi Freedom and the Global War on Terrorism.*

Naval forces also helped the Iraqi economy try to get back on its feet. Navy Seabees and Marine engineers undertook construction initiatives, building and repairing major roadways and bridges and completing major utility restoration projects. Naval EOD forces worked with the Army and Iraqi police in collecting unexploded ordnance.

With oil at the heart of Iraq's economy, the United States focused substantial effort on rebuilding its petroleum industry. The al-Basra and Khor al-Amaya oil terminals constituted key components of the industry, as they enabled Iraq to export oil by tanker and thereby to generate critical revenue. ABOT resumed operations shortly after the war; KAAOT reopened in February 2004.

Some 90 percent of Iraq's oil exports went through the al-Basra terminal, which, by October 2004, was handling about 1.6 million barrels per day. Between July 2003 and April 2004, Iraq exported 370 million barrels, mainly from ABOT.

It fell to Naval Forces Central Command to protect the al-Basra and Khor al-Amaya terminals. Combined Task Force 58, consisting of U.S. Navy, U.S. Coast Guard, Royal Navy, Royal Australian Navy, and Iraqi Navy vessels, was stood up and given responsibility for maritime operations in the Northern Arabian Gulf. Naval Mobile Security Sailors guarded the terminals themselves while coalition ships and aircraft patrolled nearby.

Between April 2003 and late September 2004, more than 120 attacks took place on Iraq's energy infrastructure, including its 4,350-mile-long pipeline system and 11,000-mile-long power grid. On 24 April 2004, three dhows pulled near the offshore terminals. As CTF-58 boarding teams sent to intercept them drew near, the dhows exploded. One of the explosions flipped over a Navy boat, killing two Navy Sailors and a Coast Guard Sailor and wounding five others. The two other dhows exploded about 50 yards from the al-Basra terminal when interception teams fired on at least one of them. The blast inflicted minor damage on the terminals, which were back in business the next day. The incident marked the first known attack on these maritime facilities since the war.

Coalition forces also dealt with piracy in the Northern Arabian Gulf. In April 2004, an armed group raided a vessel carrying Australian wheat. The ship was anchored at some distance from the port of Umm Qasr when the incident occurred. The next month, pirates armed with AK-47 assault rifles and posing as policemen attacked the crew

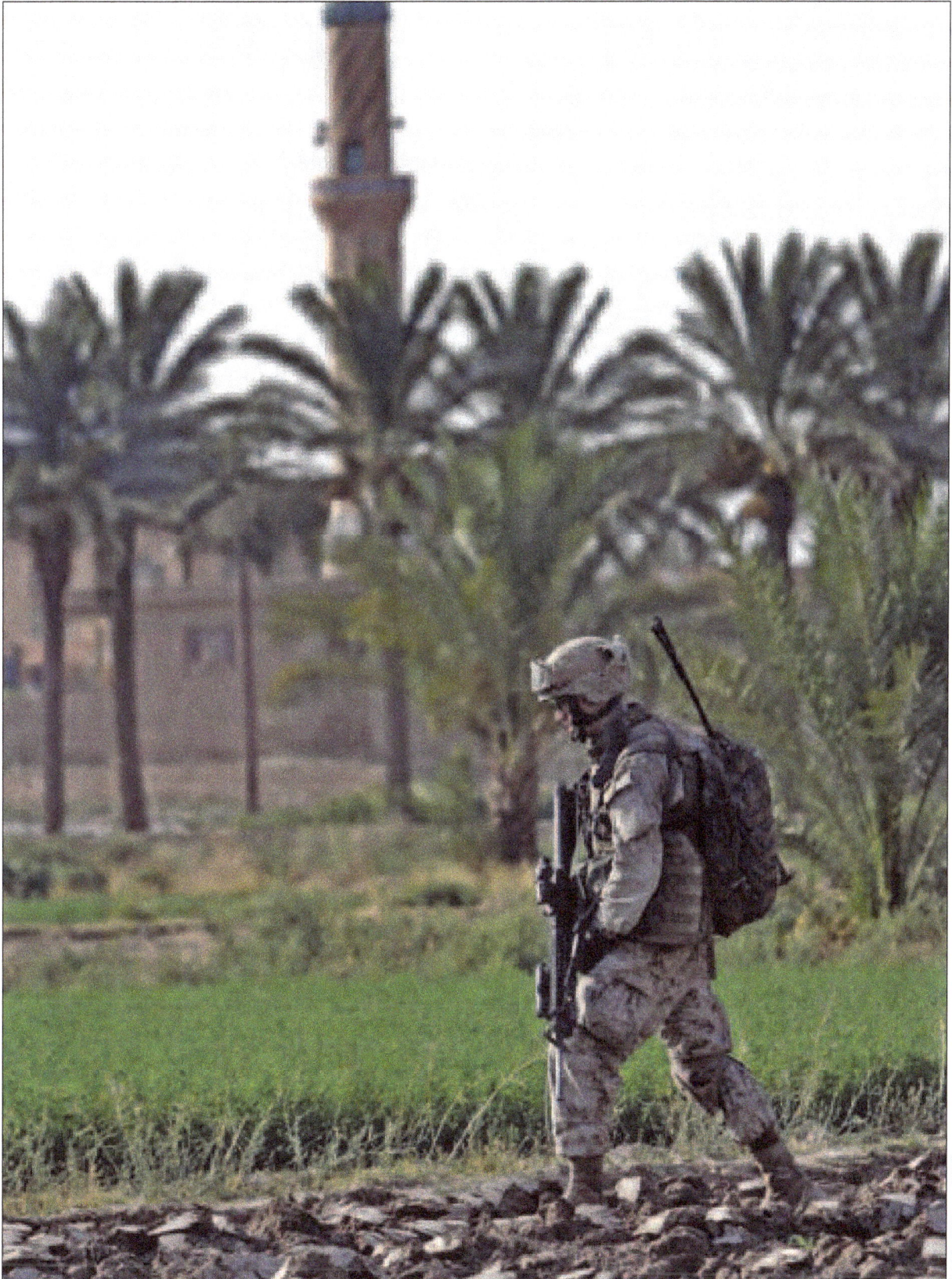

Lance Corporal Wyatt C. Zimminger patrols a palm grove in Haditha, Iraq, 11 August 2006.

of supertanker *Nord Millennium* about 10 nautical miles from the al-Basra terminal. The pirates assaulted the master and made off with money. The supertanker signaled mayday and a coalition warship soon arrived on the scene.

CTF-58's other main mission involved training Iraqi marines and the new Iraqi navy. Eventually, the Iraqis will assume responsibility for security and

"K-Dog," a bottle nose dolphin trained for EOD work, during an exercise in the Arabian Gulf, 18 March 2003.

stability in the Northern Arabian Gulf region. This mission was in keeping with the overall U.S. policy to train and equip Iraqi Security Forces capable of securing Iraq by themselves and enabling U.S. forces to draw down. "Our strategy can be summed up this

way," President Bush said in a 28 June 2005 speech, "as the Iraqis stand up, we will stand down." At that time, according to the Department of Defense, Iraqi Security Forces numbered about 169,812 members.

The new Iraqi forces included a navy numbering about 600 sailors. The Iraqi navy consisted of a patrol boat squadron and a coastal defense regiment and was equipped with donated small boats. Its mission was to patrol Iraq's waterways to prevent smuggling and infiltration. In March 2005, it took control of its own naval base at Umm Qasr, and as of July 2005, U.S. Navy personnel were turning over security responsibility for the al-Basra and Khor al-Amaya terminals to Iraqi naval forces.

Bush administration officials pointed to the successful elections and progress in developing the Iraqi Security Forces as evidence that their policy in Iraq was succeeding. Time will tell.

In April 2005, Naval Forces Central Command launched the term Maritime Security Operations (MSO) to describe its mission in the Global War on Terrorism. CENTCOM's Combined Maritime Force conducted MSO to deter terrorists from using the sea as a venue for attacks; to deny the sea to terrorists for transporting people, weapons, or other materials; and to disrupt terrorist attack planning. Maritime Security Operations set the conditions for security and stability at sea, as well as complemented regional nations' counterterrorism and security efforts. MSO embodied nearly all of NAVCENT's traditional missions: protecting sea lines of communication; engaging America's allies; conducting visit, board, search, and seizure operations; protecting key infrastructure nodes, such as the gulf oil platforms; deterring and disrupting piracy; assisting mariners in distress; providing humanitarian assistance; and conducting combat operations.

Navy Hospital Corpsman Seaman Eduardo Rivera, assigned to the 24th Marine Expeditionary Unit, provides security for his fellow Marines and Sailors as they search rooms during a cordon and knock mission outside Forward Operating Base Camp Kalsu, Iraq, 11 November 2004.

Under the MSO vision CTF-58 continued to carry out its mission in the Northern Arabian Gulf to protect Iraq's oil platforms and to train the Iraqi navy, while CTF-150 continued to secure the sea throughout its massive operating area. Another naval organization, Combined Task Force 152, patrolled the central and southern Arabian Gulf. All three task forces reported to the Combined Maritime Forces Component Commander, Vice Admiral Patrick M. Walsh, who took command of Naval Forces Central Command/Fifth Fleet in November 2005. Usually the forces involved in Maritime Security Operations numbered about 20,000 men and women and 45 ships—30 from the U.S. Navy and 15 from coalition navies, including units from Gulf Cooperation Council countries.

"We are all humans first, not Christians or Muslims," said Pakistani seaman Azad Bukhari. "As humans, our needs and wants are equal, and we all want freedom. Terrorism threatens freedom. By fighting terrorists at sea, we are an iron wall against that threat. We are saving the world from terrorism." +++

Smoke and fire belch from vehicles destroyed by an IED on a street in Baghdad, 27 August 2006. This particular blast killed two innocent people and wounded approximately thirty others.

A Marine pilot signals thumbs-up before launching from Harry S. Truman into Arabian Gulf skies, 24 January 2005.

CONCLUSION

THROUGHOUT ITS HISTORY, Naval Forces Central Command/Fifth Fleet has successfully carried out its mission to promote peace, stability, and prosperity in the Central Command area of responsibility. The Navy has accomplished this mission by keeping open the region's sea lines of communication, engaging America's allies in combined exercises, conducting VBSS operations for a variety of purposes, protecting key portions of the region's infrastructure, deterring and disrupting piracy, assisting mariners in distress, conducting humanitarian assistance operations, and, when necessary, fighting and winning.

The United States Navy followed American merchant ships into the North Arabian Sea and Arabian Gulf in the nineteenth century, when the Royal Navy ruled those waters. The U.S. Navy's presence grew as America's interests and commitments in that part of the world increased. With the establishment of the Middle East Force in 1949, the Navy became America's first line of defense in the region and the Navy's presence became permanent. With the departure of British forces east of Suez in the 1970s and the creation of Central Command in 1983, the United States Navy became the preeminent maritime force in the Arabian Gulf and Arabian Sea.

Over the next twenty years, epic sagas of human misery unfolded in Iran, Iraq, Somalia, and Afghanistan as war ravaged those lands and consumed millions of lives. Throughout this period, Naval Forces Central Command helped to mitigate the impact of regional warfare on America and its allies, as well as to alleviate some of the suffering. During Operation Earnest Will, the Navy's presence prevented Iran from inhibiting the free flow of commerce through the Arabian Gulf. During Operations Desert Shield and Desert Storm, the Navy's ability to control the sea and project power ashore proved crucial to evicting Iraqi forces from Kuwait. Throughout the 1990s, surface ships conducting VBSS operations, naval aircraft

flying patrol and strike missions in no-fly zones, submarine and surface ships launching Tomahawk missiles, and sealift vessels surging combat forces to the theater helped contain Saddam Hussein's regime, avert aggression against his neighbors, and prevent him from rebuilding a potent war machine. At the same time, naval ships and aircraft brought food to starving Somalis while naval combat forces stood by in case United Nations troops ashore needed help. During Operation Enduring Freedom, the naval forces served as the coalition's primary instrument in destroying al-Qaeda's ability to operate effectively from Afghanistan. During Operation Iraqi Freedom, the Navy played a crucial role in eliminating Saddam Hussein's regime. During the Global War on Terrorism, Maritime Security Operations denied terrorists the use of the sea and inhibited smuggling, piracy, and other illegal maritime activity. Meanwhile, U.S. Sailors in the region routinely rescued mariners in distress; provided relief to victims of floods, hurricanes, and volcanic eruptions; and participated in combined exercises designed to help America's allies provide their own security.

Since its establishment, Naval Forces Central Command/Fifth Fleet has been an anchor of resolve in the Middle East, South Asia, and East Africa, always ready to support American policy in that part of the world. +++

ACKNOWLEDGMENTS

I am fortunate to work at the Naval Historical Center, the U.S. Navy's official history agency, and I'm indebted to the leadership of Naval Forces Central Command for the opportunity to work on the exhibit and book projects. I would especially like to thank Vice Admiral David C. Nichols Jr. and Rear Admiral William E. Gortney who, as COMUSNAVCENT and NAVCENT Chief of Staff, envisioned, launched, and funded the projects. I am also grateful to Vice Admiral Patrick M. Walsh and Vice Admiral Kevin Cosgriff for seeing the book through to completion.

Other NAVCENT staff members deserve special thanks. I am indebted to Captain Jamie Graybeal and Commander Lisa Brackenbury who, as PAO and Deputy PAO, identified the Center as the logical organization to create the exhibit and write the book. I am also grateful for their hospitality in hosting Center historians during two trips to Bahrain. Thomas M. Kirby and Commander Jeffrey Breslau have my gratitude for reviewing the manuscript. I thank Lieutenant Commander Charles W. Brown and Mass Communications Specialist 1st Class (SW/AW) Katt Whittenberger for their help with photographs.

I couldn't have written this book without help from fellow Naval Historical Center staff members. I thank Rear Admiral Paul E. Tobin Jr., USN (Ret.), Director of Naval History, and Dr. William S. Dudley, former Director of Naval History, for their leadership and encouragement from the book's inception through its publication. I also thank Captains Duane Heughan and Peter Wheeler, successive deputy directors during that period. I am particularly grateful to my supervisors, Edward J. Marolda, Senior Historian/Chief, Histories and Archives Division; Gary E. Weir, the former head of the Contemporary History Branch; and Commander Gregory Contaoi, USN, for their guidance, support, and management of this project.

Many of my colleagues at the Center provided invaluable help. I am indebted to Gina Akers, John Hodges, Ariana Jacob, Allen Knechtman, Kathy Lloyd, Tim Pettit, Joel Westphal, and Wade Wyckoff of the Operational Archives, as well as Linda Edwards, Davis Elliott, Glenn Helm, Heidi Myers, Young Park, and Tonya Simpson of the Navy Department Library for research support. Sandy Doyle, the Center's Senior Editor, did her usual excellent job in preparing the manuscript for publication and guiding it through production. Morgan Wilbur, the art director of *Naval Aviation News* magazine, has my gratitude for his advice on the imagery and the layout. I am indebted to historians John Sherwood, Jeff Barlow, and Randy Papadopoulos for their constructive criticism and insights. Morgan Wilbur and John Sherwood did most of the nitty-gritty work on the exhibit panels. I thank John Barnes, Lieutenant Travis Bode, Jack Green, Jill Harrison, Ruby Hughlett, Yeoman 2nd Class Deborah Johnson, Kishia Murray, Randy Potter, Donna Smilardo, and Yeoman 1st Class Stacey Thomas, and Lieutenant Christine Tully for providing administrative support. I am particularly indebted to the men and women of the Center's Navy Reserve Combat Documentation Detachment 206 who spent many months in the field collecting records and interviewing Navy men and women so that the nation may forever remember the Navy's role in Operation Enduring Freedom, Operation Iraqi Freedom, and the Global War on Terrorism.

I am especially indebted to Captain Michael H. McDaniel, USNR, who served in Bahrain during Operation Iraqi Freedom, making the Center known to the NAVCENT staff, bringing the exhibit and book projects back to Washington, and guiding our civilians through the proper military channels to see these projects to fruition.

Most of all I want to thank the men and women in uniform who make history by their selfless service to our nation. +++

While the historical literature on America's political and military involvement in the Arabian Gulf region is fairly large, the literature on the Navy's role in the region is quite small. The following essay highlights the best works on these subjects.

Those interested in the history of Naval Forces Central Command/Fifth Fleet might want to begin by gaining an understanding of the broader context. The best one-volume history of the U.S. Navy in the twentieth century is George Baer's *One Hundred Years of Sea Power: The U.S. Navy, 1890–1990* (Stanford, CA: Stanford University Press, 1994). Albert Hourani's *A History of the Arab Peoples* (Cambridge: Harvard University Press, 1991, 2003) is the best survey of Middle Eastern history. Malise Ruthven's *Islam in the World* (New York: Oxford University Press, 1984, 2000) provides an excellent introduction to the region's predominant religion. Daniel Yergin's *The Prize: The Epic Quest for Oil, Money, and Power* (New York: Simon and Schuster, 1991) presents the best general history of the geopolitics of oil. Kenneth M. Pollack's *Arabs at War: Military Effectiveness, 1948–1991* (University of Nebraska Press, 2002) offers a good analysis of warfare in the Middle East. For a good short introduction to the background of the Global War on Terrorism, see Bernard Lewis' *The Crisis of Islam: Holy War and Unholy Terror* (New York: Modern Library, 2003). Former CIA analyst Michael Scheuer's *Through Our Enemies' Eyes: Osama bin Laden, Radical Islam, and the Future of America* (Washington: Potomac

American Sailors help off-load the British logistic ship RFA Sir Galahad *(L 3005) at the Iraqi port of Umm Qasr, 28 March 2003.* Sir Galahad *was the first vessel to deliver humanitarian assistance supplies to the port during Operation Iraqi Freedom.*

PH1 Ronald V. Woxland

Books, 2002) stands as the most insightful book on al-Qaeda.

The best introduction to the history of the U.S. Navy's presence in the Arabian Gulf region remains Michael A. Palmer's *On Course to Desert Storm* (Washington: Naval Historical Center, 1992), which covers the period through the Tanker War. Palmer's *Guardians of the Gulf* (New York: Free Press, 1992) covers the same ground, plus presents one of the first accounts of the Gulf War to appear in print. A good history of the Navy's relationship with Bahrain is David Winkler's *Amirs, Admirals and Desert Sailors: Bahrain, the U.S. Navy, and the Arabian Gulf* (Annapolis: Naval Institute Press, 2007). These books constitute the only overviews of the Navy's history in the region published to date. Otherwise, the history of Naval Forces Central Command must be gleaned largely from books written about specific military operations.

Although many books have been published about the Gulf War, most of them appeared within a year or two after Desert Storm, and therefore suffer from the pitfalls of "instant history," such as lack of perspective, narrow focus, limited access to primary sources, and polemical intention.

That said, several good books on the Gulf War have been written. The best one-volume history of naval operations in that war is Edward J. Marolda and Robert J. Schneller's *Shield and Sword: The United States Navy and the Persian Gulf War* (Annapolis, MD: Naval Institute Press, 2001). Marvin Pokrant's *Desert Shield at Sea: What the Navy Really Did* (Westport, CT: Greenwood, 1999) and *Desert*

Storm at Sea: What the Navy Really Did (Westport, CT: Greenwood, 1999) examine the Navy's role in greater detail. The best work on Desert Storm air operations is the *Gulf War Air Power Survey*, 5 volumes and a summary volume (Washington: GPO, 1993), directed by Eliot A. Cohen. An excellent official history of Army operations is *Certain Victory: The United States Army in the Gulf War* (Washington: GPO, 1993), directed by Robert H. Scales Jr. Rather than a one-volume study of the Gulf War, the Marines produced a series of short monographs. Begin with Charles J. Quilter's *With the I Marine*

Gunner's Mate 3rd Class Victoria Masako Nigorizawa cleans a machine gun during a force protection watch near the bridge of the amphibious ship Comstock *(LSD 45), 11 March 2003.*

Expeditionary Force in Desert Shield and Desert Storm (Washington: GPO, 1993). The best accounts by journalists are Rick Atkinson's *Crusade: The Untold Story of the Persian Gulf War* (Boston: Houghton Mifflin Co., 1993) and Michael R. Gordon and Bernard E. Trainor's *The Generals' War: The Inside Story of the Conflict in the Gulf* (New York: Little, Brown, and Co., 1995), although neither book says much about the Navy.

Many instant histories and good books have been published on Operation Iraqi Freedom, relatively fewer on Operation Enduring Freedom. General Tommy Franks' memoir *American Soldier* (New York:

Harper Collins, 2004) presents the commander's perspective of both operations. Benjamin Lambeth's *American Carrier Air Power at the Dawn of a New Century* (Arlington: Rand Corp., 2005) details the contributions of carrier aviation to the major combat periods in Afghanistan and Iraq, and is available online at www.rand.org/publications/MG/MG404/. A good overview of Operation Enduring Freedom is Norman Friedman's *Terrorism, Afghanistan, and America's New Way of War* (Annapolis: Naval Institute Press, 2003). The unclassified official histories of Operation Iraqi Freedom published to date include Nicholas E. Reynolds' *Basrah, Baghdad, and Beyond: The U.S. Marine Corps in the Second Iraq War* (Annapolis: Naval Institute Press, 2005) and Gregory Fontenot, E. J. Degen, and David Tohn's *On Point: The United States Army in Operation Iraqi Freedom* (Annapolis: Naval Institute Press, 2005). Michael R. Gordon and Bernard E. Trainor's *Cobra 2: The Inside Story of the Invasion and Occupation of Iraq* (New York: Random House, 2006) and Thomas E. Ricks' *Fiasco: The American Military Adventure in Iraq* (New York: Penguin Press, 2006) are outstanding journalistic accounts of Iraqi Freedom. Robert Fox's *Iraq Campaign 2003: Royal Navy and Royal Marines* (London: Agenda Publishing, 2003) is a picture book offering anecdotes on British naval participation in OIF. No other books have appeared on naval operations in the Afghan and Iraqi wars.

No books have been published on what the Navy did in the region apart from the big post–Cold War operations, a subject worthy of research. Good places to start include the bibliographies of works cited here as well as Internet search engines and online bookstores. Serious research should include bibliographies, articles published in defense journals, reports produced by the Center for Naval Analyses, and primary source materials housed at the Naval Historical Center's Operational Archives. +++

ACRONYM GLOSSARY

ABOT	Al-Basra Oil Terminal		CG	Guided Missile Cruiser
AGF	Miscellaneous Command Ship		CHOP	Change in Operational Control
ANZUS	Australia, New Zealand, United States		CINCCENT	Commander in Chief, Central Command
AOR	Area of Responsibility		CINCPAC	Commander in Chief, Pacific Command
ARG	Amphibious Ready Group		CJFMCC	Coalition Joint Forces Maritime Component Commander
ASU-SWA	Administrative Support Unit Southwest Asia		CJTF	Combined Joint Task Force
ATO	Air Tasking Order		CJTF-HOA	Combined Joint Task Force Horn of Africa
AVP	Small Seaplane Tender		COMUSNAVCENT	Commander U.S. Naval Forces Central Command
AWACS	Airborne Warning and Control System		CPA	Coalition Provisional Authority
BB	Battleship		CSG	Carrier Strike Group
CA	Heavy Cruiser		CTF	Combined Task Force
CAOC	Combined Air Operations Center		CV	Aircraft Carrier
CENTCOM	U.S. Central Command		CVE	Escort Aircraft Carrier
CFACC	Combined Forces Air Component Commander			

PHAN Flyan O'Connor

The carrier Carl Vinson *(background) relieves* Harry S. Truman *in the Arabian Gulf, 19 March 2005.*

CVN	Aircraft Carrier (Nuclear Propulsion)		MIF	Multinational Interception Force
DD	Destroyer		MIO	Maritime Interception Operations
DDG	Guided Missile Destroyer		MPSRON	Maritime Prepositioning Ship Squadron
DE	Destroyer Escort		MSC	Military Sealift Command
EMIO	Expanded Maritime Interception Operations		MSO	Maritime Security Operations
EOD	Explosive Ordnance Disposal		NATO	North Atlantic Treaty Organization
ESG	Expeditionary Strike Group		NAVCENT	Naval Forces Central Command
FAST	Fleet Antiterrorism Security Team		NGO	Non-governmental Organization
FFG	Guided Missile Frigate		NSA	Naval Support Activity
FOB	Forward Operating Base		OEF	Operation Enduring Freedom
FSS	Fast Sealift Ship		OIF	Operation Iraqi Freedom
GCC	Gulf Cooperation Council		OPEC	Organization of the Petroleum Exporting Countries
GPS	Global Positioning System		OPLAN	Operation Plan
GWOT	Global War on Terrorism		OPNAV	Office of the Chief of Naval Operations
HOA	Horn of Africa			
IED	Improvised Explosive Device		RDJTF	Rapid Deployment Joint Task Force
JCS	Joint Chiefs of Staff			
JFACC	Joint Force Air Component Commander		REFORGER	Return of Forces to Germany
			SEAL	Sea-Air-Land
JTFME	Joint Task Force Middle East		SSN	Submarine (nuclear powered)
JTF-SWA	Joint Task Force Southwest Asia		T-AO	Fleet Oiler
KAA	Khawr Abd Allah (waterway)		T-ATF	Fleet Ocean Tug
KAAOT	Khor al-Amaya Offshore Terminal		TF	Task Force
			TLAM	Tomahawk Land Attack Missile
LCC	Amphibious Command Ship		UAE	United Arab Emirates
LHA	Amphibious Assault Ship (General Purpose)		UNITAF	United Task Force
LPD	Amphibious Transport Dock		UNOSOM	United Nations Operation Somalia
LPH	Amphibious Assault Ship		UNSCOM	United Nations Special Commission
LSD	Landing Ship, Dock			
MCM	Mine Countermeasures		UNSCR	United Nations Security Council Resolution
MEB	Marine Expeditionary Brigade			
MEF	Marine Expeditionary Force, Middle East Force		VBSS	Visit, Board, Search, Seizure
			WHEC	High Endurance Cutter
MEG	Marine Expeditionary Force Engineer Group		WMD	Weapons of Mass Destruction
MEU(SOC)	Marine Expeditionary Unit (Special Operations Capable)			

INDEX

Page numbers in *italics* indicate illustration captions. Unless otherwise mentioned all ships and units are United States forces.

near Kuwait border (1995), 60; and oil smuggling, 65–69, 88; post–Desert Storm goals of, 59, 88; refuses to cooperate with U.N weapons inspections, 61–62, 88; suppresses 1991 Kurdish and Shiite rebellions, 31; takes power in Iraq, ix, 12; and terrorism, 90; and Usama bin Laden, 90; and violations of no-fly zones, 34–36, 61–62; WMD program of, 88, 90, 91

Hussein, Uday, 98

Idaho (BB 42), *38*
Illustrious (United Kingdom), 61
improvised explosive device, 107, *111*
Incirlik Air Base, Turkey, 32
Independence (CV 62), 20, 23, 33, *37*, 61
India, 51, 65
Indonesia, 75
Infinite Response, Operation, xi, 76
International Red Cross, 50
Invincible (United Kingdom), 61, 101
Iran: in CENTCOM AOR, 9; criticizes air strikes against Iraq, 62; and hostage crisis, 8, 16, 19; and oil, 1–2, 12; and Kurdish and Shiite rebellions (1991), 31; revolution in, ix, 8; and Twin Pillars policy, 7; and war with Iraq, 12–19; and World War II, 2
Iran Ajr (Iran), *17*, 18
Iran-Iraq War, 12–19
Iraq: in CENTCOM AOR, 9; and Combined Task Force 58, 108; and coup (1968), 12; Desert Storm forces of, 24; and fall of Saddam Hussein's Baathist regime, 99; and invasion of Kuwait, ix, 20, 71; and Iraq Governing Council, 104; and Iraqi Freedom, Operation, xi, 88–99; and Kurdish and Shiite rebellions (1991), 31–32; map of, 89; and massing of forces on Kuwait border (1994), 36–37; and massing of forces near Kuwait border (1995), 60; national elections in, 104, 107, *107*; navy of in Desert Storm, 24, 26, 28; and oil, 2; and oil smuggling, 65–69, 88; post–major combat operations in, 103–11; and terrorism, 72, 90; U.S. troop rotations in, 107; violates no-fly zones, x, 34–36, 61–62; and war with Iran, ix, 12–19; WMD declaration of, 91; WMD program of, 88, 90-91
Iraqi Security Forces, 110
Irbil, Iraq, 60
Ireland, Shannon, *36*
Istiqlal, 28
Italy: in Combined Task Force 150, 100; in Desert Shield/Storm, 23; in Enduring Freedom, 81; in maritime interception operations, 64; in Restore Hope, 51; in Tanker War, 15; in United Shield, 53
Iwo Jima (LPH 2), 30, *100*

Jalalabad, Afghanistan, 84
Janni, Nico, *42*
Japan, 81
Jarrett (FFG 33), 18
Jebel Ali, United Arab Emirates, 35, 46
Jeddah, Saudi Arabia, 2

John C. Stennis (CVN 74), 61, *87*
John F. Kennedy (CV 67), 24, *87*
John S. McCain (DDG 56), 69
John Young (DD 973), *18*
Johnston, Robert B., 51, 52
Joint Force Air Component Commander, 22, 34, 83. *See also* Combined Forces Air Component Commander
Joint Forces Command-East (Bahrain, Kuwait, Qatar, Oman, Saudi Arabia, UAE), 29, 30
Joint Forces Command-North (Egypt, Kuwait, Saudi Arabia, Syria), 29, 30
Joint Task Force Middle East, ix, 17–19
Joint Task Force Southwest Asia, x, 33
jointness, 16–17, 33–34
Jordan, 9, 31, 72
Jubaland, 53
Jubayl, Saudi Arabia, 23
Juffair, Bahrain, ix, 4, 7, 44
Juneau (LPD 10), 51

Kabul, Afghanistan, 73, 75, 84, 87
Kandahar, Afghanistan, xi, 74, 85
Karachi, Pakistan, 101
Karbala, Iraq, 31, 97
Karzai, Hamid, xi, 103
Kashmir, 75
Katz, Douglas, 38, 40
Kazakhstan, 10
Kearsarge (LHD 3), *99*
Keating, Timothy J., 81
Keffer, Jonathan, 66
Kelso, Frank B., 38
Kelley, P. X., 9
Kenya, xi, 9, 57–58, 76, 102
Khafji, Saudi Arabia, 26–27
al-Khalifa, Isa bin Salman, 6, 7
al-Khalifa, Salman bin Hamad, 6
al-Khalifa, Salman bin Hamad bin Isa, *45*
Khartoum, Sudan, 76
Khawr Abd Allah waterway, 65, 66, 69, 95
Khobar Towers, Saudi Arabia, x, 43–44, 73
Khor al-Amaya Oil Terminal, 94, 108, *108*, 110
Khomeini, Ayatollah Ruhollah, 8, 12
Khost, Afghanistan, 76
Khuzestan Province, Iran, 12
King, Ernest J., 41
Kingston, Robert C., 8
Kitty Hawk (CV 63), 35, 81, 84
Kurds, 31–32, 60, 98
al-Kut, Iraq, 98
Kuwait: in CENTCOM AOR, 9; in Desert Fox, 62; and Desert Shield/Storm, 23; in Desert Thunder, 61; in Determined Response, 77; Iraqi invasion of, ix, 20; map of, 21; and maritime interception operations, 64; and oil, 1, 2; in Restore Hope, 51; and security pact with U.S., 54; and Tanker War, 14–15, *15*

Oil-for-Food Program, 59, 65, 69
O'Kane (DDG 77), 69
Okinawa, Japan, *38*
Okinawa (LPH 3), *14*
Oldendorf (DD 972), 47
Oman: in CENTCOM AOR, 9; and Combined Task
    Force 150, 101; and Desert Fox 62; and Determined
    Response, 77; and maritime interception operations, 64;
    and terrorism, 72
Omar, Mullah Muhammad, 74
1 (UK) Armoured Division, 92, 94
I Marine Expeditionary Force, 27, 29, 30, 92, 94, 97, 98;
    Engineering Group, 98–99
101st Airborne Division, 85
OPEC, 59
operations. *See* Anaconda; Arabian Gulf, carrier operations;
    Desert Shield; Desert Storm; Desert Fox; Desert
    Strike; Desert Thunder; Determined Response; Earnest
    Will; Eastern Exit; Enduring Freedom; humanitarian
    operations; Iraqi Freedom; Infinite Response; leadership
    interception operations; maritime interception
    operations; maritime security operations; Northern
    Watch; Praying Mantis; Provide Comfort; Provide
    Relief; Resolute Response; Restore Hope; Sea Angel;
    Southern Focus; Southern Watch; Unified Assistance;
    United Shield; Vigilant Sentinel; Vigilant Warrior
Operation Enduring Freedom maritime interception
    operations, 100–101
Operation Plan 1002-90, 20, 22
opium poppies, 72
Organization of African Unity, 50

Pacific Fleet, 16, 17, 38, 41. *See also* U.S. Pacific Command
Pahlavi, Muhammad Reza, 7–8
Palestine, 2
Palestine Liberation Organization, 90
Pakistan: in CENTCOM AOR, 9; in Combined Task
    Force 150, 100, 101; and Enduring Freedom, 85; in
    Provide Relief, 50; in Restore Hope 51; and smuggling,
    65; soldiers killed by Somali militia, 52; and support
    for Afghan Mujahidin, 70, 71; and the Taliban, 74; in
    United Shield, 53
pan-Arabism, 12
Pashtuns, 74
Paul F. Foster (DD 964), 22
Peacock (sloop), 1
Pearl Harbor (LSD 52), 101
Peleliu (LHA 5), 48, 84, 85, 107
Pentagon, xi, 78, 80
Perry, William J., 41
Persia. See Iran
Peshmerga, 98–99
Peterson (DD 969), 36, 69
Philippines, 75
piracy, 108–9
Plant, Amy, *50*
Poland, 23, 61, 64, 93, 94

Port Royal (CG 73), 87
Portugal, 23, 150, 100
Powell, Colin, 23
Praying Mantis, Operation, ix, 19
preemption strategy, 90
Prima Maersk (Denmark), 47
Prince Sultan Air Base, Saudi Arabia, 82
Princeton (CG 59), 29
Provide Comfort, Operation, x, 31, 32, 60
Provide Relief, Operation, x, 50, 52
Puntland, 53

al-Qaeda: and Enduring Freedom, 84, 87, 100; founding
    of, 70–71; in 9/11, xi, 78; post–major combat operations
    against, 102–3; pre-9/11 operations of; x, xi, 72–73,
    75–77
Qatar, 2, 9, 54, 64, 77
Quincy (CA 71), ix, 2, 3

Ranger (CV 61), 24, 51
Rapid Deployment Joint Task Force, ix, 8, 9
Ras Tanura, Saudi Arabia, *xiii*, 4
Rasheed military airfield, Iraq, 98
Ready Reserve Force, 11
Reagan, Ronald, 9
Red Crescent, 50
Red Reef, Exercise, 55, 58
Redd, Scott, 40–41
Reforger, Exercise, 54
Rendova (CVE 114), 6
Republican Guard (Iraq): in attack on Irbil, 60; and defense
    of Kuwait 24; deployment of near Kuwait border (1994),
    36; in Desert Fox, 61–62; in Desert Storm, 30; in invasion
    of Kuwait, 20; in Iraqi Freedom 96, 98
Resolute Response, Operation, 76
Restore Hope, Operation, x, 51–52, *52*, *53*
Rivera, Eduardo, *111*
Riyadh, Saudi Arabia, x, 22, 40, 72
Rogers, David N., 33, 38
Romania, 61
Roosevelt, Franklin D., ix, 2, 3
Royal Navy, 1
Royal Saudi Air Force, 55
Royal Saudi Naval Forces, 55
Ruble, R. W., *viii*
Rumaila oil fields, Iraq, 94–95
Rumsfeld, Donald, xi, 87, 92, 102, 104
Rushmore (LSD 47), 51
Russia, 1, 62, 92. See also Soviet Union

al-Sabah, Jaber al-Ahmed al-Jaber, 90
Sabha (Bahrain), *57*
Saddam Canal, Iraq, 97
Saddam International Airport, Iraq, 98
al-Sadr, Moktada, 104
Said, Saiyid, 1
Saipan (LHA 2), 99

Incoming Commander Task Force 150, French Navy Rear Admiral Alain Hinden, left, reports to Vice Admiral Kevin Cosgriff during a change of control ceremony, 4 April 2007. Cosgriff took command of NAVCENT on 27 February 2007.

www.ingramcontent.com/pod-product-compliance
Lightning Source LLC
Chambersburg PA
CBHW050644150426
42813CB00054B/1176